CONNECTICUT CHARACTERS

For Steve,
Thanks for
coming out and
supporting me —

Randy Beard

CONNECTICUT CHARACTERS

Profiles of Rascals and Renegades

RANDALL BEACH

Globe
Pequot

Essex, Connecticut

Globe
Pequot

The trade division of The Rowman & Littlefield Publishing Group, Inc.
4501 Forbes Blvd., Ste. 200
Lanham, MD 20706
www.rowman.com

Distributed by NATIONAL BOOK NETWORK

British Library Cataloguing in Publication Information available

Library of Congress Cataloging-in-Publication Data

Names: Beach, Randall, 1950- author.
Title: Connecticut characters : profiles of rascals and renegades /
  Randall Beach.
Description: Essex, Connecticut : Globe Pequot, [2023]
Identifiers: LCCN 2023002929 (print) | LCCN 2023002930 (ebook) | ISBN
  9781493071814 (trade paperback) | ISBN 9781493071821 (epub)
Subjects: LCSH: Connecticut—Social life and customs—Anecdotes. |
  Connecticut—Biography—Anecdotes. | New Haven register (New Haven,
  Conn. : 1961)
Classification: LCC F94.6 .B43 2023 (print) | LCC F94.6 (ebook) | DDC
  974.6—dc23/eng/20230120
LC record available at https://lccn.loc.gov/2023002929
LC ebook record available at https://lccn.loc.gov/2023002930

♾™ The paper used in this publication meets the minimum requirements of American National Standard for Information Sciences—Permanence of Paper for Printed Library Materials, ANSI/ NISO Z39.48-1992.

To all these wonderful characters who generously gave their time and attention to me in order that I could tell their stories.

Contents

CONTENTS

CONTENTS

Introduction

Here they are—my favorite local characters as I brought them into the eyes and imaginations of *New Haven Register* readers from 1980 to 2020.

Really? I was at this for 40 years? Although these columns spanned that period, you will notice there were gaps, including from 1984 to 1987, when I left New Haven and did freelance writing in Boston and elsewhere. Another hiatus occurred from 1989 to 1998, during which I pursued other work, including editing a new nostalgia magazine, "Remember," in Norwalk, Connecticut.

But something always drew me back to New Haven and its compelling people. There's nothing more fulfilling than finding a unique, interesting and unknown person, interviewing him or her and bringing that personality out of the shadows and into the public eye.

Randall Beach's wife Jennifer Kaylin at a promotional billboard, circa 1988. (Photo by Randall Beach)

Although from the very beginning I sought out those previously unknown individuals, I also seized the chance when it arose to write about celebrities such as "Little Richard," Yale University President A. Bartlett Giamatti, the writers Kurt Vonnegut and Hunter S. Thompson, and Red Sox pitching ace "Smoky Joe" Wood.

Sometimes the people I chose to highlight were a little too odd for some of my editors, colleagues and readers. I recall that after I wrote about "Brother John," a homeless man who panhandled on the Yale campus, my editors didn't understand why I gave him "the ink." In the early years of my column, then called "At Large," other Register reporters called it "creep of the week." They asked me: "Who's your creep this week?"

I would usually laugh it off. But sometimes I'd offer this: "They're not 'creeps.' They have great dignity. Their stories deserve to be told."

Nobody hands you anything in journalism, and the idea of writing my own column didn't come from any of my editors. I had that goal in mind for many years before I saw my chance in the fall of 1980. For a long time before that I read and admired the columns of Red Smith and Russell Baker of the New York Times, Jimmy Breslin of the New York tabloids and Bob Greene of the Chicago Tribune. I said to myself: "One day I'd like to have a newspaper column."

I saw an opportunity when the *New Haven Register*'s Bill Ryan stopped writing his "Roamin'" column. I noticed he wrote well, apparently about anything he wanted to, and seemed to be having a fine old time.

Soon after Ryan left the *Register* I approached the editors with a proposal: in addition to continuing my coverage of New Haven as a general assignment reporter, I would give them a column once a week about a colorful local person. I knew my chances for a "yes" would be greatly diminished if I asked for more money to do this. And so I didn't even suggest it. (Indeed, a raise was never offered.)

The editors thought it over and said: "Sure, kid, give it a shot."

I immediately got in touch with Gerald Forde, a kind, intelligent and funny elderly man-about-town who went to murder trials at the New Haven courthouse for entertainment and stimulation. As I spoke with him for that first column, I learned about his early life in Ireland witnessing the Irish Civil War.

My columns drew an enthusiastic response from the *Register*'s readers. It was clear they enjoyed hearing about the people I was bringing into their homes. And so I kept going.

Through those years I was often asked: "Where do you find all these people?" Many of them I discovered during my roamings and ramblings. But many others were suggested to me by the readers. They knew they could trust me to write about my subjects with some insight and empathy. I tried never to mock anybody, no matter how eccentric he or she appeared to others.

As I write this introduction all these years later in 2022, it's gratifying to know that these characters—many of them now deceased—will again have their moment in the sun. Enjoy!

Violent Past is Still Vivid
in Irishman's Mind

(November 15, 1980)

WHILE AMERICANS HIS AGE WERE LEARNING READING, WRITING AND arithmetic and playing cowboys and Indians, 12-year-old Gerald Forde was learning how to throw hand grenades, fire a revolver and ambush British soldiers.

Fortunately, he never had to use his deadly knowledge, although he often witnessed brutality during the Anglo-Irish War and Irish Civil War in the 1920s. Forde immigrated to the United States in 1929, settled in New Haven and pursued a peaceful life of literature, poetry and non-violent activism.

Forde was forever marked by his childhood—inspired by Irish resistance to the British and saddened by what he calls "the dark side of human nature."

He still refers to his young years as "those terrible days." He remembers them so vividly that, like a veteran of other wars, he has nightmares about it to this day.

GERALD FORDE
Remembers the "terrible days"

Gerald Forde. (*New Haven Register* file photo)

While Forde cannot agree with the provisional Irish Republican Army's present-day tactics which often kill civilians, he still admires his family members who fought the British Army and staged hunger strikes after being imprisoned.

"They were my heroes; they surely were. They're still my heroes, when I think what they went through. I could never explain to you the great patriotic feeling there then."

Recalling his childhood in a stream of consciousness, Forde completely entranced a group of teachers at a Hillhouse High School workshop. Between tales of bravery and grief, he recited poetry and sang songs of the resistance. The memories have not faced—nor has his Irish accent.

"I was supposed to give a talk," he said apologetically. "I don't fancy that too much—I do suffer from stage fright. And I don't pretend to be a singer. But I'm a better singer than my prominent namesake is a statesman."

After sitting speechless for a few minutes in a desk at the head of the classroom, looking like a kid who wanted to escape the teachers' clutches, Forde began: "I was born on a farm in County Leitrim, in the west of Ireland. What happened there influenced all the rest of my life. When I was 10 years old, in one week I learned three wonderful lessons which were for the good.

"I remember being at Mass this particular Sunday when we heard a commotion at the door of the church. I looked up and there were six British soldiers walking down the aisle, battle helmets on their heads and rifles in their hands. They were looking for IRA men on the run.

"Children started to cry; they were terrified, including myself. I remember so vividly when the priest heard the commotion, he looked around, put his hands out and said: 'Don't be afraid—just let the devil come forward.'

"Ever since then, I've admired moral and physical courage."

After the Mass ended, Forde returned and learned another lesson: "I remember looking down the aisle of the church, seeing an English soldier kneeling down, devoutly praying. While his comrades were across the street in the public house, drinking and carousing, he had the moral courage to go into the church and kneel down and pray. And since then, I realized that in this world there's really no black and white. I also learned the lesson that enemies are people.

"The following Tuesday, as I was getting up to go to school, all across the countryside I heard the roar of mortars, horses' hooves and shouted commands. This was known as a round-up. The British Army came slowly in, in a circle, and every man under a certain age was taken into custody.

"Near the end of the day, two soldiers came across the field to our house. My father, who was hale and hearty, had the presence of mind to do something I really admired him for, his quick thinking. He grabbed two sticks and limped out to meet these soldiers. My sister and I stood in the doorway, laughing our heads off.

"My father wasn't an educated man, but he was an intelligent man; I think there's a difference. He used to tell us the most important quality any man could have is common sense."

Several days after the round-up, Forde was sent to County Meath to live with his uncle, who was a priest. "The intention was that I would become a priest too. It didn't work out that way, but that's another story.

"My uncle and his housekeeper had a great love of reading and music and poetry. They instilled that in me, and I have it still to the present day.

"But I had an aunt who married into a family with eight brothers. Three of those brothers were actively involved in the fight for independence. They took part in ambushes, were interned in camps for years and went on hunger strikes. They taught me another side of life.

"Instead of teaching me how to play football or hurling, they taught me how to throw hand grenades. I very well remember one of them telling me emphatically, 'When you pull the pin with your mouth, be sure to count to six. Don't count over six or it'll explode in your hand. And if you throw it too soon, it can be thrown back before it explodes.'

"I thought this was great. And they also showed me in diagrams how to organize an ambush of a military convoy on a country road."

Forde said one of his cousins was killed when the British mounted a counter-ambush. Forde sang a song written after that battle, recounting how the Irish fighters "were shot down like partridges in clover."

"So here's to Bern Baxter, the O'Reillys, O'Connor and McCabe,
Who gave up their friends, home and life's blood,
And died that their dear land might be saved."

Forde paused. "The last name in that, McCabe, he was my cousin."

Forde said the British Army customarily avenged IRA ambushes by "going around the farmhouses, burning them down, shooting up the nearest village. And at the time they had reinforcements: an infamous group called the Black and Tans. The English were determined to put down this insurrection, so they recruited ex-convicts and gave them a fabulous salary. There weren't enough uniforms to go around, so they gave them black police jackets and tan Army pants.

"These Black and Tans struck terror into the hearts of the people, just as the Gestapo did in the hearts of the people of occupied Europe years later."

One day when he was alone in a farmhouse with his aunt, Forde saw the Black and Tans in action. The family had been harboring an IRA leader, who took a chance by going to a football game to watch his old school play.

"And he was betrayed. He tried to run, but he was riddled with bullets. The Black and Tans put his body in a truck to bring him back from town. Outside my aunt's house they stopped the truck, jumped out and started dancing and throwing their berets in the air, shouting, 'We got fresh meat here! We got fresh meat here!'"

Forde learned early on what happened to informers. He came to Mass one Sunday and saw a man tied to the gate of the church, tarred and feathered. A sign pinned to him said: "Spies and informers beware."

"Evidently his crime wasn't too severe," Forde said. "Others were shot. But it's rather sad how some people will sell their souls for money, how a man will betray his comrades."

His uncle was once called upon to witness a "confession" of this sort. "In the middle of the night a school teacher and three masked and armed men came into my uncle's house. They had an informer with them, and they took him up to the mountain in back of the parochial house to hear his confession. After that, my uncle gave him communion and the last rites, and they shot him."

Forde asked his uncle: "Father Michael, when will this horror stop?"

The priest replied, "Gerald, as you go through life, remember two things: This too shall pass, and nothing matters much."

In light of his childhood experiences, Forde said, "I have great empathy for the children of Northern Ireland and the children in the Palestinian camps and in Afghanistan. I know how it will affect them the rest of their lives. It affected me to a great extent. I think for one thing it made me very much of a rebel. It made me question authority and so forth."

Forde became a union activist when he took a job with the New Haven Water Co. after coming to America. "Some people in the company tried to crucify me. But I never gave up.

"I'm glad I came here because the freedom in this country is wonderful. That's *political* freedom. But sometimes you don't have economic freedom. That's why I joined the union."

Forde also protested the Vietnam War and was tear gassed in New Haven during the 1970 May Day disturbances. "I often think it's too bad that 'the best and the brightest' in America didn't consider how guerrilla warfare was successful in Ireland before we plunged into that terrible tragedy in Vietnam."

Now retired, Forde takes in many guest lectures at Yale, literary discussions in churches and even murder trials in New Haven Superior Court. "I like the drama. It's better than going to a play or movie. Anything can happen."

Although he occasionally sings Irish ballads for charities or speaks before the Irish History Round Table in Hamden, Forde says, "I'm an introvert trying to be an extrovert. I'd rather stay home and read books."

Lincoln is One of a Kind to Its Faithful Movie Buffs

(February 7, 1981)

YOU MIGHT CALL THE LINCOLN THEATER AN ENDANGERED SPECIES. BUT it's not a species at all—it's one of a kind.

The last of the neighborhood movie houses, the Lincoln (on Lincoln Street between Orange Street and Whitney Avenue) has a colorful history. Its precise genesis remains a mystery.

But movie buffs don't much care what it was—they're delighted with what it is. Count me among them; one of the reasons I moved to Trumbull Street was to have the Lincoln Theater in my backyard.

When some people go to the movies, they climb into their cars, risk life and limb on I-95, endure tolls and fumes, and pay large sums of money in order to see a first-run film in a conglomerate that looks more like a world's fair pavilion than a movie theater. And after they pay their admission they have to sit through commercials.

When I'm in the mood for a movie (Bogart, Woody Allen or a foreign film), I walk around the corner and plop down three bills ($2 for students and senior citizens). The grouchy bald-headed guy in the ticket window mumbles and tears a stub off his roll, like a man operating the roller coaster at a carnival.

The place is so small that it can't help but be cozy and intimate. The lounge, reached through a door down the aisle, is wonderfully funky, with faded furniture and map-of-the-world wallpaper.

Ah yes, memories of Sunday matinees in the Lincoln on a rainy day, watching an Alfred Hitchcock double bill. Rain pounds on the roof—and eventually splatters onto the floor, sometimes onto your face. You can't buy this kind of atmosphere anywhere. It's better than Cinerama.

Unfortunately, the roof was recently fixed. This is bad news for the old man who used to come in on Sunday afternoons when the sun shone through the hole above, throwing a spotlight on a particular seat. He claimed that seat as his own. "When the sun hits me on my bald spot," he said, "it warms me up."

Robert Spodick (left) and Leonard Sampson in their Lincoln Theater. (*New Haven Register* photographer John Ewing)

Sure, some facets of the Lincoln aren't so charming. It isn't quaint or lovable when the projector breaks and the screen goes dark in the middle of a gripping scene. This is an occupational hazard of the place.

But you always get two movies—and some of the pairings are inspired. Where else could you see Mae West's "I'm No Angel" and W.C. Fields' "The Bank Dick" back-to-back? The winter film festival also features Charlie Chaplin's "Modern Times" and "Monsieur Verdoux," "All That Jazz" and "The Rose," "Cabaret" and "The Blue Angel." For those with warped tastes, the Lincoln for several years offered the ultimate test of viewer endurance: John Waters' "Pink Flamingos" and "Female Trouble" on the same bill.

Robert Spodick and Leonard Sampson, who lease the theater from the City of New Haven, have been told the building was originally a stable. As for the middle years, Spodick once discovered blueprints dated 1924 which indicated Yale's drama school used the structure for plays, under the name of the Little Theater Guild of New Haven.

7

The Lincoln became a movie house in the 1930s and was owned for six memorable months by Joseph E. Levine, now a big-name producer. Levine titillated his audiences by showing gangster films, interspersed with such stimulating shorts as "Reefer Madness" and "How to Undress Before Your Husband."

Spodick and Sampson, self-described as "bright-eyed boys managing theaters in New York," came to New Haven in 1945 and leased the Lincoln from Morris Nunes and Maurice Bailey. The city took it over in the mid-70s; Spodick and Sampson stayed on, paying rent, continuing to show foreign films and old-time classics, while waiting for the Redevelopment Agency to give the go-ahead for a new Lincoln Theater on Audubon Street.

They're still waiting.

"We're in limbo," said Spodick. "The city has abandoned the parking garage idea, which was what the project hinged on."

That's no tragedy for people who love the Lincoln. Under the redevelopment plan, the old place would be murdered by the wrecker's ball.

"Some people want to get landmark status for it," Spodick said. "We told them, 'Don't do us any favors.' It's all right to be quaint; charm and nostalgia and all that. But we've got to do something. We've done some patching up but you can see we need new seats and a new projector. The roof needs to be insulated. It's just bare boards. If we knew we were going to be here for a few more years, we could do more to fix up the place."

While they wait for news, any news, on the city's plans for the neighborhood, Spodick and Sampson sit upstairs in their cluttered office, surrounded by photographs of Doris Day, Julie Andrews and other celluloid heroes.

"We have a place to come to here," said Spodick. "We do have a tremendous attachment to it."

Yet there's no profit to showing revivals. Spodick and Sampson are able to keep the Lincoln going only because of their proceeds from the York Square Cinema and the Crown Theater, which they own.

"We don't make a nickel here," said Sampson. "We're just hanging on until we see what happens."

3

Exit's Return Brings Back Folk Music

(February 28, 1981)

RANDY BURNS BELIEVES THE TIME IS RIGHT FOR AN ASSAULT ON THE "bourgeois." No, it's not 1962, but in this dreary winter of 1981 he has resurrected The Exit coffeehouse.

The original Exit, still spoken of affectionately by Burns and other "folkies" who populated it, closed nine years ago for lack of money and crowds. But for 10 years (1962 to 1972) it was a mecca for people who felt they didn't fit anywhere else.

Three nights ago Burns and two Yale students launched the new Exit in a game room at the university's Jonathan Edwards College on High Street. The place was packed. Students sat at candle-lit tables or on floor mats, softly singing along with a series of folksingers. There was a bit of the old magic.

Burns, pleased by the turnout, plans to continue the experiment on Wednesday nights (9 p.m. to midnight). Although non-students are welcome, he hopes to make the Exit more of a community gathering by eventually finding a place off-campus. (New Havenites may now pick up Exit invitations at Viva Zapata, 161 Park Street.)

The old Exit, initiated by young members of church groups, moved around from Wall Street to Chapel Street to the basement of First United Methodist Church.

"It was a wonderful place," said Burns, now 32, as he sat at the Viva Zapata Bar, currently his favorite hang-out. "Anybody who had anything to do was there. Great performers, all playing for nothing.

Folksinger Randy Burns. (*New Haven Register* file photo)

"Those were great days—great for creativity, great for music. The trouble with The Exit was you thought the rest of the world was going to be like that too."

Burns now makes his daily bread by playing at Zapata, Maggie's and some of the more trendy nightclubs, which have recently come to town, such as West of Eleven and New Haven on Chapel Street.

"Every new place that opens in this town seems to be bourgeois," he said. "People sit around in leisure suits, sipping $2 drinks. But you've got to play for them, if you want to make a living.

"Do you believe they've got a computer bar? You press a button for the gin, a button for the tonic . . ." He shook his head.

"The days of the good old saloon are gone; places where you could go and be whatever you wanted to be."

Another blow to the saloon scene was the passing of Jocko Sullivan's several years ago. Burns had been a mainstay there, singing and helping to bring in acts such as John Hammond and Tom Paxton. It's been redecorated and is now called Kavanagh's. There are potted plants in the window.

"That was a good joint," Burns mused. "We had some good nights there."

But Burns insists he is not hung up on the past, is not trying to relive his youth with his attempt to bring back The Exit.

"We have a new, right-wing administration. Inflation is killing everybody. Every time inflation hits, it seems people need entertainment. They hit the beer halls.

"All you have in New Haven is pop-rock. Bands doing Aerosmith, Beatles, Fleetwood Mac—that's all you hear in this town. We've got to get something original. It's worth a shot."

Burns decided a long time ago that writing and singing music was what he was going to do. At age 16 he picked up his guitar, ran away from his home in Higganum and headed straight for Greenwich Village. Its cafes were filled with the sounds of young singers such as Bob Dylan and Phil Ochs.

"I was lucky. I got hired as the permanent opening act at the Gaslight Café, playing with John Hammond, Mississippi John Hurt and all the other old folkies.

"Everybody helped everybody else. There was no jealousy. People helped each other get jobs rather than trying to stay aloof, like they are today."

Burns landed a record contract and put out six albums. A new thing happened to his life: money started rolling in. "I spent it all, every dime of it."

In 1973, he stopped recording. "I was just sick of it. An executive came in and said, 'Let's hear your new songs.' Instead I played sea chanteys and old Irish ballads. The guy said, 'I love those songs but if you want to play that, we'll have to release you.'"

Burns returned to New Haven. His parents weren't thrilled by his progress.

"My mother would say, 'Why don't you learn how to fix cars or paint houses?' But I've always been scared to death that if I got locked into a situation I liked and fell in love with somebody, I might end up constantly doing that job because I'd need the money to keep all that. That's why I've never learned how to do anything. I'll be damned if I'm going to get hung up like that. If I'm not making money singing I don't want to make it any way else."

He said his parents still aren't thrilled. "They'd be happy if I got a job, something respectable. Ever since I quit my job at the car wash, they knew I was going downhill."

Burns has survived by accepting generosity ("I'm not a chauvinist—I let women support me") and by adopting a frugal lifestyle. He has no telephone, no car, just walks everywhere. He lives across the street from Viva Zapata, within walking distance of his clubs.

He's accompanied at most of his shows by "A.J." (Alan John Mulhern), who has been his faithful sidekick for the past 11 years. They harmonize.

Although he surprised his friends last year by going to Los Angeles and writing songs for a "New Wave" band, Burns hasn't written anything in six months. "I write in spurts. I'll write five or 10 songs in two days. I read where one musician said, 'I don't have any respect for someone who doesn't write every day.' That guy should've been an insurance salesman. He could work 9 to 5. You write when you've got something to say. Otherwise you'll write crap."

Burns admits to a certain amount of fantasizing about what might have been. He recalled how folksingers replaced rock 'n' rollers until the rockers learned to "say something" in their music, too, and knocked the folkies out. "We taught them too well. We could've lasted another five years—then I would've been a star."

But Burns says he's no more nostalgic than the next guy, and is convinced the future holds as much excitement as the '60s. "I've always felt that something else is gonna happen. If this (the new Exit) doesn't work, something else will. I couldn't stay in this business if I didn't have optimism."

4

"Little Richard" Born Again

(October 24, 1981)

"Little Richard" is still an entertainer. But instead of singing rock 'n' roll he's singing and preaching in churches.

He doesn't sing "Tutti Frutti" or "Good Golly Miss Molly" anymore. But he knocks crowds out with his soulful rendition of "God's Beautiful City."

He still calls himself "Little Richard," although now he's introduced as "Evangelist Little Richard." And his show is such a crowd-pleaser that he packed them in during a three-night stand last weekend at Faith Seventh-Day Adventist Church in Hartford.

They got fire and brimstone. Richard, sweating heavily, roamed around the stage, jumped onto the floor, worked the crowd, exhorting the good people about the sins of drugs and homosexuality.

He's an authority on these topics. He's been there.

"I went from marijuana to angel dust, from angel dust to cocaine, from cocaine to heroin. After falling into the drug trap I became a world-famous homosexual. I didn't realize the devil had put me there."

"Amen!" shouted a woman in the congregation.

"God made men to be men and God made women to be women! There's no in-between.

"Is this too nasty to talk about? Somebody's got to do it. Somebody's got to tell the world it's a sin."

"Thank you for the truth, Richard! Praise the Lord!"

"That's why God called me—he needs someone to talk about these things. Some people say 'Little Richard' has no discretion. I imagine that's what they said about John the Baptist."

The organ music began and Richard went into his prayer. "I know there are many people here tonight who would like to overcome rock 'n' roll music, who would like to overcome homosexuality. Come forward. Don't let the devil keep you in your seat. Won't you give your life to Jesus?"

As Richard sang gospel, the people came to him. He hugged

"Little Richard." (*New Haven Register* file photo)

them and blessed them. Then another preacher reminded the audience that it had cost Richard a lot of money to fly to Hartford from his home in California. And for the second time that night, ushers passed buckets down the pews.

"Put something in those buckets," Richard called out. "Help 'Little Richard' as I travel the world for Jesus. How many of you can give 'Little Richard' $100 tonight? You gave it to me when I sang 'Tutti Frutti.'"

Indeed they did. He claims he made "$10,000 an hour" at the height of his success as a rock 'n' roll pioneer in the '50s. Many music historians trace the very beginning of rock music to his immortal shout kicking off "Tutti Frutti" in 1955: "A WOP BOP ALU BOP, A WOP BAM BOOM!"

"I know I started rock 'n' roll," he said during an interview in the pastor's study. "There wasn't no Elvis then. Chuck Berry was singing the blues."

Where did it come from? What inspired it? "It just came overnight. I developed it from gospel."

The Beatles often acknowledged their debt to "Little Richard" and he thinks that's only right. "The Beatles got their start from me. I am Paul McCartney's idol." He whipped out a photo of himself surrounded by the foursome. "This was taken in 1960."

Should he have gotten more credit and more money? "Definitely I should have! The Beatles had a lot more money behind them. My manager couldn't afford a cup of coffee."

He put away the photo. "But it doesn't matter now. I'm not looking for any credit because I'm a child of the King. I went from rock 'n' roll to the rock of ages."

5

"Smoky Joe" Heats Up For Fenway Start

(March 27, 1982)

MORE THAN A HALF-CENTURY AFTER HE PITCHED HIS WAY TO GLORY for the Boston Red Sox, Westville's "Smoky Joe" Wood will return to Fenway Park to try out the old pitching arm.

It's hard to believe that the Red Sox owners have only now gotten around to inviting Wood back. But on April 12, the Sox season home opener, this will be rectified.

Wood, now 92, sat contentedly in his home on Marvel Road, contemplating the return of baseball. It's been a long winter. Football, basketball and hockey just don't do it for him.

Has he ever thrown out the first ball at any baseball game? "Yeah," he laughed. "Little League!"

Better late than never. He's pleased that the Red Sox asked him to do it. "There's a great part of the United States doesn't know I'm still alive."

But there's a great part that does. "Some kid just sent me a baseball to sign," he said. Asked if this happens often, he acknowledged, "Oh, I get cards and baseballs just about every day. They remember."

Yes, they remember (or they have read) that in 1912, the year Fenway Park opened, Wood won 34 games and lost only five. That included a streak of 16 consecutive wins. With Wood's help the Red Sox made it to the World Series that year and beat the New York Giants, four games to three. Wood won three of those four games.

The next year he broke a thumb in his right hand (and he was a righty). But he still had some good years left in his arm, notably in 1915 when he won 14 and lost five as the Red Sox won another World Series.

After a contract dispute with the Red Sox, he was traded to the Cleveland Indians where he became an outfielder. Then in 1922, though still a fine player (he hit .366 in 1921), he grew weary of life on the road and decided to settle down and get to know his kids. He accepted an offer to coach baseball at Yale and he's lived in New Haven ever since.

Many baseball fans are outraged that despite his achievements and records, Wood was never voted into the Hall of Fame. But he said gruffly, "I don't feel it'd be a great honor to be

"Smoky Joe" Wood at his home in New Haven, March 1982. (*New Haven Register* photographer Gene Gorlick)

there. There are many guys there who we didn't even consider good players in my day. No, I have no interest in it whatsoever."

His 1916 contract dispute was small potatoes compared with the sums paid today's player-millionaires. On the radio the day we visited Wood, the big news in the baseball world was that Los Angeles Dodgers pitcher Fernando Valenzuela had grudgingly shown up for training camp, ending his protest over being offered only $350,000 to throw a baseball this year. He wanted $850,000.

Guess how much Wood was paid at his peak—$7,500. The dispute arose when the Red Sox wanted to cut his salary by $2,500.

But Wood doesn't begrudge today's players their astronomical earnings. Of Valenzuela, he said, "I think he's just smart. He's got a good agent; all the players these days have them. They load that place (Dodger Stadium) every time he pitches. Why shouldn't he get it?

"The owners got the money in my day. They took it all."

Wood had no opinion to offer on last year's strike by the players. But he said, "I missed it a great deal, yes. That's what I do—just listen to baseball.

"I lost my wife three years ago this August. My daughter and her husband, they've got an apartment upstairs. It's a very nice arrangement."

He got up to take down his wife's picture from the mantelpiece. "This is what she looked like when I first met her in 1908. That's when they wore those big hats."

Then he pulled out a gold pocket watch. "I've carried this now for 66 years." The inscription reads: "To Smoky Joe Wood, in appreciation of his splendid pitching which brought the World Championship to Boston in 1912."

"Here's what they gave us for the 50th reunion in 1962," he said, taking down a gold electric clock. "Oh, it's stopped—no, it hasn't . . . When they gave these to us, only nine of us from the 1912 team were living. Since then, all of them have died but me."

6

Gina Tickles Memories and Keys at Old Barge

(August 28, 1982)

"Hey Gina! Play that piano! You sexy thing!"

It's a Friday night, just before 9 p.m. Gina, sitting at the bar of the Old Barge Café on Front Street in Fair Haven, drains her drink and stubs out her cigarette. It's time for her to go on.

Smiling at the gibes from the loud-mouthed customers, she heads for the piano. She is dressed in a red pantsuit, her work clothes.

She sits down at the piano, pauses a moment, then breaks into the opening bars of "New York, New York." Mitch, a young regular with a "Rock of Ages" tattoo on his right bicep ("That's from the first chapter of the Bible"), raises his head and smiles. He sidles over to the piano and starts to "harmonize" with a good ol' boy wearing a cowboy hat who is feeling even less pain than Mitch.

Together, the three of them produce an unforgettable sound.

Gina is a beloved figure at the Barge but she remains a lady of mystery. Few of the regulars know much about her. She won't give out her last name to anybody, for reasons of her own. But she can play that piano.

Every Friday, Saturday and Sunday she performs whatever the customers request. And they don't just sit there and listen; they sing along. If they don't know the words, they fake it.

Sometimes they dance across the old wooden floor of the converted oyster barge. On many nights an ageless wonder named Eldridge, sporting a Red Sox cap, shows up with his spoons and plays alongside Gina. They make beautiful music together.

"I've been coming here for years," said a middle-aged man in one of the booths near the piano. "But after all this time singing and listening to Gina, I never learned her full name, and she doesn't know mine. I'm president of a local bank."

Between songs Gina eventually revealed a bit of her past. Born in New Jersey, learned to play piano at age six by listening to her older sister. Took lessons from a blind professor in Bridgeport. Graduated from high school at age 15 and received her master's in music from Boston University at 16, which is still a school record.

"My father was a well-known opera singer in Italy. I definitely inherited some of his musical talent. So did my sister—she sings opera on Long Island. But I never heard my father sing. He died when I was three."

Her stepfather, recognizing Gina's natural skills, convinced a school to donate its piano to her. "He brought it home in a wheelbarrow."

Her first performing job was at the amusement park in Revere Beach, Mass. She was 18. Then her family moved back to Bridgeport, so she played at nightclubs there. She's played at so many clubs and weddings over the years that she can't remember them all. But since coming to the Barge six months ago, she's found a home.

"Of all the places I've played, I like this the best. People are friendly here, they appreciate me. I feel very well-respected, well-liked. I enjoy the singalongs, which I never had before. I used to play by myself.

"I've had offers to play nice, high-class places but I like ordinary people. Here, I don't feel I'm being snubbed by anybody."

Does she have any regrets over not being in the big time? "I'm not looking to be famous. I've always been the shy type. When I was younger I did have a chance to go to Europe and study with my uncle. Now, I wish I'd gone. But I was too timid."

Despite the repeated requests for familiar songs ("My Way," "Roll Out the Barrel," "Daisy," "Take Me Out to the Ballgame"), she never tires of them. "I like to please the public. Whatever they enjoy hearing, I enjoy playing."

She plays Frank Sinatra with special warmth, feeling a kinship with him because, she said, ol' Blue Eyes baptized one of her distant relatives. "But I do opera too. Classical music is still my favorite."

Much later in the evening, with the strains of "Moon River" wafting out over the misty Quinnipiac, the Old Barge felt like it was drifting out to sea. Amid the applause, somebody shouted out, "Play it again, Sam!" And she did.

7

An Up-and-Down Life
Suits Solly Just Fine

(January 22, 1983)

WHEN SOLLY NODELMAN WAS A KID, HE LIKED TO COME DOWNTOWN TO New Haven to ride the elevators.

"I'd watch the operators, notice their habits, how they used their hands," he says.

There are only a few manually operated elevators left here now, but Nodelman runs one of them. Four mornings a week at the City Hall building on Church Street, he offers an alternative to today's automated elevators.

A machine can't shoot the breeze with you. Nodelman can. And how.

"A nice soft landing on No. 1. You got it! How's that?"

"Beautiful. Like a helicopter," murmurs a happy bureaucrat.

In steps another customer, carrying a folder he's got to deliver.

"What'll you try for?" Nodelman sings out.

"Take me to the top of the park."

"You got it!"

How can this guy be so happy, day after day, ride after ride, floor after floor?

"Everybody asks me that. They say, 'You're the only one who gives a smile.' It's a habit, that's all."

He's 73 years old. "I been doing this 11 years, going on 12. I'll keep it up 'til I can't do it no more. To get up and go at this stage, it makes you feel good. To me, this is recreation. It is."

He says this is the good life, especially compared with his old job at Nodelman's News Depot near the corner of Church and Chapel Streets. He and his brothers sold newspapers, candy and tobacco and ran a shoe-shine stand.

"We closed it down around 1970. All my brothers got sick on me. It was a risky business, being there all those late hours. It was aggravation."

Now he's got no aggravation, just a lot of friendly riders. Many of them remember him from the depot days. Mayor Ben DiLieto, for instance. Nolelman notes, "He always tells the same story: how he used to keep warm downtown in my place when he was a patrolman. There wasn't much else open late at night."

Nodelman has a faded newspaper clipping on the wall of his elevator with a photo of the newsstand. Since he always runs the elevator on the extreme right side of the lobby, he's decorated it as someone would a private room or office. The other clippings are warnings about the dangers of smoking and a news photo of Jerry Lewis leaving a hospital after heart surgery. Lewis is vowing never to smoke again.

Nodelman feels badly about all the cigars he sold over the years. "I kept telling them, 'Smoking is no good for you. Why do you do it?' Whenever I see an obituary I remember what they smoked. So many people who aren't here today."

A few minutes later, a woman gets on at the fifth floor. She is smoking a cigarette. Nodelman says nothing, delivers her to the lobby.

He smiles and shakes his head. "She can't get out of the habit, she says."

Everybody's talking about the weather. Nodelman happily accommodates them, exchanging lore about winter clothing, the forecast, the coming "heat wave."

"I enjoy the people the most," he says during a free moment. "They like to come in and chatter. I go right along with them. All the people in the building are very nice. I'm satisfied. I've got no complaints."

He takes personal pride in his elevator. "I listen to it. I know when something's wrong. You get an ear for an elevator, like you do for a car.

"When I got it 11 years ago, this thing was wobbly. I thought it was me, but then I got it fixed. It runs like a Cadillac now. It's easy to handle."

He can think of only one or two buildings in New Haven that still have manually-operated elevators. "Second National Bank just went automatic," he says, as if announcing the death of an old friend.

"People don't like those things, they tell me that. Some people are afraid to ride alone. They'd rather have somebody to talk to."

8

James E. Close Is Gone:
"What're Ya Gonna Do?"

(April 16, 1983)

The Heyl & Lynch Pharmacy is dark now. There's a sign in the window—"Store for sale"—and another one telling why: "Closed due to death of James E. Close."

It was a shock to see that. James Close has been a fixture in this Orange Street neighborhood, working tirelessly in his old-fashioned shop on the corner of Pearl Street. He came to the store in 1948 and never left. In 1970, he became the sole proprietor.

Through the years neighbors came to depend on Close simply because he was so dependable. He stayed open seven days a week, walking over from his home on Clark Street every morning to sell newspapers, toothbrushes, pens and pencils, candy and cigarettes as well as pharmaceuticals.

The place never seemed to change either. Although the soda fountain was taken out about 20 years ago, that wasn't Close's doing. Once he took over he resisted "trends" and "improvements" content to fill prescriptions, shoot the breeze with customers and sell his basic supplies. He even kept an old scale by the door—you could put a penny in and weigh yourself.

His store was like something out of an old movie, set in a small town where everybody knew everybody else. He greeted by name almost everyone who walked in there. His appearance and voice were reminiscent of Spencer Tracy.

"He made that neighborhood special," said a long-time customer. "He was the village pharmacist—a nice, simple, unassuming little guy who saw himself doing a public service.

"He was a remnant of the old days when you could work your way up and buy a little storefront. You could tell he loved it when people came in and he used it as a kind of gathering place. It was *his*. Today these people are being blown away by the big chain operations. Jim Close was the druggist equivalent of a good dinner."

But this customer, who asked not to be named, recalled the day several years ago when things started to go badly for Close and his little pharmacy. "I was living in the apartment house across the street at the time. I heard glass breaking and then shouting. A kid came running out of the store and took off down the street. Jim Close tried to run after him but it was hopeless. He was robbed repeatedly after that. I think they were after his drugs.

"They never got much from him or seriously injured him but he was very unnerved. I think he was hurt more than anything else, that someone would do this to his little place. I think he felt betrayed."

His daughter Mary Close said one intruder wrapped a wire around Close's throat. "Thank God he was able to get free. He never gave them anything. They were after his drugs but he wasn't about to give that up."

She said he didn't complain about the break-ins. "He would always say, 'What're ya gonna do?' That was his favorite expression.

"He was never one for a lot of materialistic things. He just kind of let things stay as they were. Occasionally I'd suggest something but he'd say, 'It's all right the way it is.'

"He loved his work. That was his whole life. He enjoyed the customers and the kids who came in."

She and a family friend, Richard Nuzzo, are trying to sell the business. They hope it can continue as a pharmacy. Nuzzo has been going through the store records and what he has found says something more about Close.

"We discovered he was giving prescriptions at cost or below cost. If he charged a customer $5 in 1969, he'd still charge $5 in 1983. He had customers he'd been taking care of there for 30 or 40 years. I guess he never wanted to go up on them."

9

"Oldest Elvis" Keeps Shaking Pelvis

(June 18, 1983)

ELVIS IMPERSONATORS WILL COME AND GO BUT THERE IS ONLY ONE Elvis Presley—and there is only one Johnny Romano.

He isn't a household name—not yet—but if you travel the gong show club-circuit you might catch him doing his "Hound Dog" act.

"They call me 'Johnny Romano, Superstar,'" said the modest entertainer as he sat at a table at Westward Ho in Milford on a recent Thursday night, waiting to do his act. "I've been doing Elvis since I was 19.

"Now I'm almost 50 years old and I'm still doing Elvis. I'm the oldest Elvis in Connecticut. I love him. He's my boy."

Romano never met Presley, nor did he see him perform live. "But I seen him on TV. I wrote to him for an audition but I never heard back from him."

Westward Ho is a romantic spot for Romano because that's where he met his wife, Gail ("Starfire"). Yes, they fell in love at a gong show.

"I'm a talent scout," said Gail. "I was right here in this club one night in 1981, looking for local talent. At the time I met Johnny, I thought he was just another Elvis impersonator. I didn't know how wrong I was.

"This is a love story too. That night he asked me to be his manager. I said, 'I have no money, no car, but I'm willing to take a chance.' Then we started going steady. On our wedding night (July 9, 1982) we did an Elvis show at the Holiday Inn. We tore the place down.

"It's guys like Johnny that are keeping Elvis alive."

When he's performing, Romano wears an elaborate white suit with "Elvis" embroidered across the back. He has six of these outfits, all designed and made by Gail.

But the Romanos are getting tired of doing gong shows. After all, they've been at it for nearly three years. That can get to be depressing.

In order to pay their bills they wash cars. "What else am I gonna do?" Romano asked. "You could say I'm a professional car waxer in the day and an Elvis impersonator at night.

"And I'm versatile. I also do Al Jolson, Jerry Vale, Tom Jones, Perry Como. Where else can you get a guy that can do all that stuff? I've played 40 clubs—40 clubs! I played Atlantic City. I met Miss Utah, Miss Germany . . ."

"Someday this is gonna be a book," Gail said. "'The Secret Life of Johnny Romano, His True Story.' How does that grab you?"

"Max the agent," sitting at Romano's table, tried to give the budding star some expert advice. "Don't overdo it!" he cautioned. "Don't push the act!" That's like telling Ahab not to catch a whale.

The gong show had begun but Romano, befitting a star, refused to go on until other acts had warmed up the crowd. The first entrant was another Elvis impersonator, "Rick Presley." He sang "Hound Dog" and was given solid scores of 9, 9 and 9 by the judges. Ten is a perfect score.

Gail, who is a dancer and singer as well, went up next. "I'm gonna do 'It Had to Be You'—because that's how I feel about Johnny Romano."

"Max the agent" winced as she sang. When Gail finished, the guitar player accompanying the contestants said, "I think you just invented some notes that never existed." The judges gave her a combined score of 14.

Johnny's turn. He started flexing, then leaped up, grabbed the microphone. "Ladies and gentlemen, I'm doing this for my wife, Starfire. Uh one, uh two—goin' to a party in the county jail . . ."

Romano tore into "Jailhouse Rock." His legs were rubber, his arms akimbo as he did his knee splits, never missing a beat. His hips shaking, he belted out the lyrics, propelling the band and amazing the non-regulars in the audience. They'd never seen anything quite like it.

Unfortunately, the judges had. Apparently they're also tired of having Johnny Romano at the gong show. They gave him scores of 2, 7 and 8—that adds up to 17. He had been beaten by another Elvis impersonator.

Johnny Romano. (*New Haven Register* photographer
Mara Lavitt)

Romano was outraged. "Are you kiddin' me? I was gypped. They have the same judges here every week. How ya gonna win with those lousy judges? I gotta get up there and kill myself, for what?"

As he stared into his beer and a desperate woman warbled "You Light Up My Life," "Max the agent" scolded, "You never listen! You always overdo the act!"

But Gail believes her Johnny's day will come. Then places like Westward Ho will come begging for his talent. "Someday," she said, "they're gonna be sorry."

Earl's Old "Dirty Shoe" Restaurant Being Shined Up

(December 24, 1983)

EARL BAIRD'S OLD "DIRTY SHOE" DINER ON ROUTE ONE IN GUILFORD IS being cleaned up. Karen's Restaurant will now be Jimmy D's. It had to happen someday.

For at least 25 years, Baird ran the place by himself, sleeping on a cot in the back room, lounging with friends and customers in easy chairs in the big living room, which was also the dining room and restaurant.

He rarely left the building. You could count on him to be in at any hour, to shuffle out and cook you a hot dog and shoot the breeze. He said "truck drivers with dirty shoes" could find comfort there.

The message above his old grill read: "When you're in the doghouse, you're always welcome here."

Then about a year ago a strange and unfamiliar sign appeared in the window: "Closed—Please Call Again." And there the sign remained, for months.

Earl Baird had had a stroke.

He was in the hospital for a long time. He lay in bed, frustrated, knowing his loyal customers were peering confusedly through the window of his old place, seeing the grill, the chairs, the piano, the piles of magazines, everything just as before. But no Earl.

Earl Baird at Karen's Restaurant. (*New Haven Register* photographer Kirby Kennedy)

Finally he was well enough to move to Marotta Manor, a convalescent home in Guilford. But he wasn't—and isn't—able to reopen his restaurant. Someone else will have to carry on.

He is Jim Dombkowski, 20 years old. He can remember sitting in Karen's when he was a toddler, watching Baird at the grill and listening to the men talking and joking as the eggs fried.

But Dombkowski wants some changes made. "It's got a bad reputation. This used to be a hang-out for kids and truckers. It's real cleaned-up now, not like it used to be. No chairs, no nothing."

However, Baird still owns the building and he has some say over what happens to his legacy. Most mornings he gets a ride from the convalescent home to the restaurant. He watches as Dombkowski fixes up the interior.

Earlier this week Baird showed us around the place, which was still being readied for reopening. It was early morning; Dombkowski hadn't arrived.

First Baird insisted on giving a tour of the land itself. It was about 21 degrees outside but he ambled around his property with a walking stick, showing the water and gas lines. "I'm not bad for an old man, am I?" (He is 71.)

Then he showed us where he used to sleep, the tiny back room behind a door that says "Office." He hopes to move back there soon but he's unclear on exactly when or how.

He walked into the big room, the room where for decades he cooked, sat, relaxed, talked, listened to customers as they chatted and played the piano.

Today the room is sparse, cold. The piano is still there but little else remains. The chairs and piles of magazines are gone. The ambiance of a living room-tag sale joint is missing.

The old jukebox waits patiently in a corner. Through the faded glass you can barely read the titles: "Cab Driver" by the Mills Brothers, "Danny Boy" by Ray Price. Next to it, a yellowing thermometer, reading "Say Pepsi Please." In the other corner, near the grill, is a dusty phonograph.

The kitchen area has been stripped clean too. The knickknacks are gone—including the "doghouse" sign.

Baird looked around at the room for a minute, then spread his arms. "This is all mine. As long as I'm alive, this is all my property."

His eyes grew moist. "I built this place. I built it and named it for my daughter. This is a nice place. I made it for her."

A few minutes later, Karen appeared. She lives upstairs with her children. As Baird started worrying aloud about where he would live, what would happen to the restaurant, she said, "Don't worry, Daddy, everything's going to be all right." They embraced.

When Dombkowski arrived, immediately there was tension in the air. He and Baird argued about whether there should be some chairs in the room besides the customer stools.

"There won't be any chairs in here," Dombkowski said firmly. "It's gonna be run like a regular restaurant. It's not gonna be like it was."

In a few minutes Baird simmered down. "He's a good kid," he said, watching Dombkowski work. "Good luck to you, kid."

Nick Apollo's Forte is Stardom Now

(February 11, 1984)

NICK APOLLO FORTE, SUPERSTAR, WAS CHOPPING WOOD IN THE BACK yard of his unpretentious home in the shadow of Waterbury's Holy Land.

He looked up with an impish grin and bellowed a greeting for his latest visitor. Another reporter had come beckoning, asking to speak with the man who only a few weeks ago was a struggling lounge singer, a fixture on the marquees of Holiday Inns and Howard Johnsons from Meriden to New Haven.

Now he's on marquees across the country, right underneath Woody Allen and Mia Farrow. Allen's new movie, "Broadway Danny Rose," features Forte singing his own music and portraying Lou Canova, described as "a dumb, fat, tempermental has-been with a drinking problem."

The movie hasn't made it to New Haven or Waterbury yet, but the word-of-mouth is excellent; critics are raving about the film and the debut of Forte. "Awesome chutzpah," declared the Newsweek reviewer after watching Forte's performance.

"I never thought I'd be a movie star," Forte said as he finished stacking his wood. "But that's the power of music—when Woody heard my tunes, he went bananas!"

Allen's talent scout, assigned to track down an ethnic singer in his 40s, had plucked Forte's album, "Can I Depend on You," from an obscure bin in a New York record store.

So one day in July 1982, the scout called Forte and asked: "Can you meet with Woody Allen?"

Forte had barely heard the name. He'd never seen a Woody Allen film and was naturally a bit suspicious about the offer. But he agreed to meet him.

"After we talked a while, Woody looked at me and said, very softly, 'Nick, could you make a movie with me?' I said real softly back, 'Yeah, no problem.'"

They began filming in September of that year. Although Forte was working with some of the biggest stars in the business, he claims he wasn't at all nervous. "I'm an entertainer, so I had no problem playing an entertainer. But I'm not a drunk; I had to play the part of a boozing, overweight, Italian, baby, finger-clicking, egotistical kind of maniac!

Nick Apollo Forte at Ristorante Luce in Hamden, December 2006. (*New Haven Register* photographer Arnold Gold)

"It was fun. I'd never done a movie before."

Now he's getting calls, not just from reporters but from friends and relatives. "They say, 'Nick, you *are* that movie!'"

However, Forte hasn't gotten around to seeing it yet. "I would like to see it, I will, when I can sit quietly and watch it as a whole—not just (the performance of) Nick Apollo Forte."

He had moved inside, plopped down on his couch, his ample frame shifting around, his shoes off, toes wriggling, mouth giggling. Over in the corner, next to Forte's piano, his old dog Charlie snored, oblivious to his owner's sudden fame.

Forte was having a great time. "The *New York Times* is doing a story on me. So is *People* magazine. Everyone's saying, 'The world wants to see this guy now.' I'm lining up talk shows. The casting people from other movies are calling and asking me: 'Are you available?' Sure I am."

Nevertheless, Forte said he's taking it all in stride. "I'm a very calm type of guy. I don't get too excited. I like to be a regular guy, just walk into a place and have a burger."

Forte won't say what he was paid for the movie but he did buy a fishing boat he's very proud of. He named it "Scungilli."

He doesn't go for talk of "fate" or "luck." "You could say I paid my dues. Did they find my record by luck? I put that record in that store. You've got to work at it. You can make things happen."

Forte, now 45, has been working at it since he was 12. "I started as a drummer, playing in nightclubs for exotic dancers. Oh, those hula-hula girls! They brought my eyeballs out!"

There were less glamorous jobs along the way. "When I was 16 I delivered cow manure. I've sold pots and pans, worked in a shoe store."

Meanwhile, he remained in his native Waterbury, got married and raised seven kids. Playing the club circuit, he used various names, including "Nicky Redman" because his hair was so red then.

Forte said he picked up the "Nick Apollo" name in 1957 after playing the Apollo Theater in New York. "I had second billing to Della Reese. She had the big record; I had the flop. But I brought out a record every year since then. You've gotta keep the coal in the fire! I recorded on my own label, printed a thousand of them at a time. Most of the time I never sold a thousand."

However, he did have a following. "The people of New Haven especially have always been very good to me. They're gonna see this movie and say, 'That's our Nick! He's a movie star now.'

"I've played in more clubs over the years—let's not mention any names 'cause they might've gone out of business! I love that!" (Forte was laughing so hard he nearly rolled off the couch.) I closed a lot of places!"

He leaped up to put on one of his albums, "Images." It contains the two songs now in the movie, "My Bambina" and "Agita" (Italian for acid indigestion, which Forte is subject to).

"See, Italians are born with music," Forte said, dancing around and singing with himself to his composition "Robin's Song": "Keep Italian in your heart, let it always be a part of you . . ."

35

12

A Special Person is Gone and We Are the Poorer

(March 1, 1987)

NEW HAVEN, YOU HAVE LOST A VERY SPECIAL PERSON. AND I HAVE LOST my best friend. I want to tell you about him.

Eddie Petraiuolo III loved this life. He played with it, exalted in it. I've never seen anyone else light up a room like he could, simply by walking into it.

When he walked down the street, he couldn't get more than a block without greeting someone he knew. Then he'd shake hands, shoot the breeze, gather information.

If he had lived, one day he would have been mayor of this city. We used to kid him about it; I'm convinced it would have happened.

But he wasn't a calculating political sort—his idol was John Belushi, his favorite movie was "Animal House."

It was Ed Petraiuolo who, waving a sword above his head, charged out to the 50-yard line of the Yale Bowl at half-time, dressed as the Marquis de Lafayette in honor of Lafayette College, his alma mater.

He wasn't supposed to be on the field but he didn't care. As he successfully infiltrated the Dartmouth marching band, dancing around them, thousands roared in delight.

And it was Ed Petraiuolo who had planned to recruit his countless friends to charter a boat and cruise down the Nile River in Egypt on New Year's Eve, 2000 to greet the new century.

Edward Petraiuolo III. (Photo by Jennifer Kaylin)

He really would have done that. Instead he spent his final New Year's Eve lying in bed, watching an Alfred Hitchcock movie ("Rebecca") on a VCR and coughing.

Never once did he express bitterness or anger during his heroic 11-month battle with chemotherapy, radiation and surgery.

He just said he had gotten "a bad break."

When he returned home from a grim visit with his doctor in early January and told us he was going to die, he apologized in the next breath. "Sorry, guys." He felt he had let us down.

Five days before his death he hauled himself out of bed and, in an awesome display of will and courage, attended a two-act play ("Self Defense") at Long Wharf Theater. He could barely walk but he was determined to get out of that bed and go out. He made it through the entire play and seemed to enjoy it.

That was his last stand, his final night out of his apartment. Perhaps he knew he had only a few days left.

We have been cheated more than we can ever know. We'll never see another like him.

13

One Final Ride For Zonker,
a Magical Friend

(August 16, 1987)

YOU WON'T READ ABOUT HIM ON THE OBITUARY PAGE BUT SOMEBODY special recently passed away on a hot summer's day in New Haven.

Zonker, who gained nationwide acclaim as the dog who loved to ride roller coasters, will never ride again.

"The heat got to him," said Zonker's lifelong companion, Joe Barna, 38. "I asked him to wait for me when I went away on my trip. But he just couldn't make it."

What a life it was! From the day in 1978 when he first leaped aboard the Wildcat at Lake Compounce Amusement Park in Bristol, the white Keeshond's fame grew.

He was featured on the national TV shows "That's Incredible!" and "Fantasy," riding that coaster with a blissful, excited expression.

Barna always considered Zonker his "fantasy dog" come true. "He was on the 'Fantasy' show for his 100th ride on a coaster," Barna said. "And my fantasy was to have a dog that could go anywhere, off-leash. I wanted to travel, to explore the country. I wanted to hitchhike with him."

And that they did, crossing the U.S. 13 times. Sometimes they would fly (when called west for Zonker's TV appearances) or use Barna's car. But when nothing else was available Barna would stick out his thumb as Zonker sat patiently at his feet.

Zonker the wonder dog and Joe Barna ride the Wildcat at Lake Compounce Amusement Park in Bristol. (*New Haven Register* photographer Michael F. O'Brien)]

"I called him 'my four-legged insurance.' It's slower but safer hitch-hiking with a dog. It was never dull. There was always someone to talk to and play with. At night he'd curl up at my back instinctively. If he heard any noise, he'd yip to warn me."

Zonker was named by members of the Yale football team (Barna drove their bus) in honor of the "Doonesbury" character.

"In that strip Zonker is a magnificent, unbelievable character," Barna said. "In the same way Zonker was more than a dog. He managed to do things above the ordinary. He was the one who jumped into the coaster. I'd never thought of it."

Barna, who works for a Guilford computer company that assists arts projects, has devoted years of his spare time to researching and preserving roller coasters and their settings.

"I used Zonker to get publicity for the older endangered parks. I was manipulative about it, but not the way Ollie North was."

Barna said that over the past few years, "I dropped coasters as an obsession" because of work and personal commitments. But when he traveled through the Soviet Union in June and July as a photographer for the Yale Russian Chorus, his interest in roller coaster history again took hold.

"Coasters started in Russia, or the idea did, in ice slides. I took pictures of some of those old slides at a museum!"

Unfortunately, this was one trip on which Zonker couldn't come along. Barna left him with a roommate. When Barna returned, he didn't see Zonker's dinner dish by the door and he knew his old friend was gone.

"His death is a symbol of the loss of a lot of things in our society," Barna said. "The people who owned the parks used to say, 'I'll take responsibility; you can ride with your dog.' Now everybody has to use seatbelts and harnesses because of insurance problems.

"Zonker was a symbol of a time when you could live your own life. What has happened to the world that we can't do something creative like that anymore?"

Barna buried Zonker in a wooded area of Vermont "where we used to play. I built a box for him and took him up there. I put a few things in the box with him—a jug of water from a nearby fountain, a piece of wood from Lake Compounce . . ." Barna choked on his next word. "I don't think I can talk about this."

Zonker was 14 years and four months old when he died. "He came into my life cleanly, magically. He lived a wonderful life; he died easy. We should all live a life as lucky as that."

14

Alan Abel Wins Few Votes
but Lots of Laughs

(August 30, 1987)

WHEN ALAN ABEL RECEIVED ONLY 38 VOTES AS A WRITE-IN CANDIDATE for the recent 4th Congressional district special election in Fairfield County, he complained, "People don't take me seriously."

This, from a man who elaborately faked his own death so he could read his obituary in the *New York Times;* launched a campaign to "clothe naked animals for the sake of decency;" and staged a wedding ceremony using for the groom a man who was a dead ringer for deposed African dictator Idi Amin.

"I like to get people all riled up," said the 62-year-old Westport humorist-author-lecturer and self-described provocateur as he sat in the caboose in his back yard.

"That's how satire's supposed to work. It's my veiled protest against absurdity. That's always been my forte—provoking people."

The caboose, which Abel received for giving a speech to a railroaders' group in Newark, New Jersey, was used as his campaign headquarters.

He delighted in bringing unsuspecting reporters inside, then surreptitiously activating a tape of a whistling train planted underneath the bed.

"They'd look around and wonder, 'Are we taking off?'" Abel recalled, laughing at his prank.

But this was small potatoes compared to the other stunts he's pulled off. His greatest achievement has to be fooling the revered *New York Times*.

"I have a group of people I call 'my merry pranksters,'" said Abel, borrowing a phrase from California writer-guru Ken Kesey ("One Flew Over the Cuckoo's Nest"). "When I need support and money (for a hoax), I go to them.

"I guess we're all obsessed with what'll happen to us after we die. I was able to tune in and find out. It was quite a learning experience."

His death required $3,000, imagination and great attention to detail.

One of his pranksters set up a "funeral home" out of a trailer near Orem, Utah and even got a phone listing. This friend also ventured out to Sundance (actor Robert Redford's ski lodge) and planted a pair of skis in the snow. The stage was set.

Meanwhile, an actress friend of Abel's, posing as "the grieving widow," burst into the *Times* office that Sunday night and tearfully reported the death of her "husband," replete with documents of his achievements.

A *Times* reporter called the "funeral home," where Abel's buddy confirmed his death. The diligent scribe also called a New York church where a spokesman truthfully asserted that yes, it has been booked for a wake for Alan Abel.

"I got six inches, six nice paragraphs!" Abel said proudly. "I stood in the snow on 57th Street in New York—I was hiding out in an apartment there—and read my obituary. Talk about 'The Twilight Zone.'!"

His other exploits include a "females for felons" campaign wherein actresses volunteered to minister to inmates; and the fake unveiling of "Deep Throat," the source who broke open the Watergate scandal.

"It's amazing that people will buy these cockamamie stories," Abel said.

Abel has a lot of other pranks in mind but lacks the necessary capital.

"We were going to land a Martian on the shores of New Jersey, but we ran out of money to build the spaceship. I'd still like to do it someday. I'd also like to look for the Loch Ness monster—or if there isn't one, dump one in the lake."

He said these stunts are "therapeutic," a way to deal with rejection—rejected manuscripts, movie ideas. But he has managed to publish several books, including "Don't Get Mad . . . Get Even!" With his wife Jeanne he also co-wrote a movie script that was accepted and filmed: "Is There Sex After Death?"

"The trouble is, people get to be 21, turn 'adult' and they're told to throw away their toys and get serious," Abel said. "I've never accepted that. You have to have fun and laugh at things, because the world is ridiculous."

15

Maurice Bailey Put the "Show" in Showmanship

(October 25, 1987)

MAURICE H. BAILEY IS GONE AND SO IS THE GLORIOUS ERA WHEN HIS Shubert Theater was "The Birthplace of the Nation's Greatest Hits."

We hardly knew him. Bailey, who died 10 years ago, was a dedicated public servant but an intensely private man who never gave a newspaper interview in his life.

However, we have here the next best thing—a treasure trove of memories shared by Bailey's widow Lilyan, with a supporting cast of two of his daughters and his private secretary.

Lilyan, 81, still lives in downtown New Haven. Robert Spodick, co-owner of the York Square Cinemas, aptly describes her as "the grand dame of New Haven's film and theater scene."

She met Bailey in 1926. "I was attracted by his mind, his heart, his compassion for people. He was really a very unusual man."

His family immigrated to America from Russia when Bailey was four. As a boy he began to sell the *New Haven Register*. He was so good at it that he eventually acquired a horse and buggy for delivery and hired other people to sell more newspapers. This helped him pay his way through Yale.

One of his daughters, Ginger Begun, said, "Daddy delivered papers to 'the ladies.' That's what he called the prostitutes."

"He said they were hot tippers," chimed in another Bailey daughter, Rita Gwin.

Bailey was notoriously cautious with his money but in 1941 he saw an opportunity he couldn't refuse: managing the Shubert Theater. The Shuberts were then under government pressure to divest themselves of the theater because of a monopoly charge.

Lilyan said Bailey successfully resurrected the sagging Shubert because he was "a dynamic man." Edie Goodmaster, who was his personal secretary for 25 years, said, "He was a great businessman."

They noted Bailey served for 23 years on the city's Board of Finance, where he was known as "the watchdog of the treasury." But he was generous enough to help build the Jewish Home for the Aged of New Haven and the B'nai Jacob Synagogue in Woodbridge.

Bailey also operated a chain of movie theaters—among them the Whalley, the Whitney, the Strand and the Crown—but the Shubert received most of his attention.

His duties sometimes required deft psychology—especially the night he convinced a young Rex Harrison, stricken with stage fright, that the show ("My Fair Lady") must go on.

Goodmaster recalled: "Mr. Bailey told Harrison's manager: 'OK, we'll tell the newspapers and radio that the show is canceled because Mr. Harrison is afraid to go on.' The manager said, 'Wait a minute' and Harrison agreed to do the show. That was Mr. Bailey's uniqueness—he knew where to go, what to do."

Lilyan added, "Rex Harrison never gave a performance as brilliant as that night. He got a standing ovation."

Lilyan also vividly remembers the night Mae West came to their home. "She asked, 'What would you like to hear me sing?' And she sat down at the piano and a metamorphosis took place. This little demure person began to wriggle and shake. It was delightful."

Lilyan said Bailey was offered many show business opportunities elsewhere but he always turned them down "because he loved home. He was a sentimental slob but he didn't want anybody to know it."

In 1977, amid hard times for grand old theaters, Bailey was forced to close the Shubert. "He was too ill to fight it," Lilyan said. Two months later, he died.

She has been back only once to the restored Shubert; she can't believe there isn't even a plaque there for her husband. "The only room they didn't disturb was the auditorium. And I couldn't stay there. It was too much . . .

"It's sad. It was a beautiful era."

16

In His Heart He Knows He is Santa Claus

(December 20, 1987)

Yes, Virginia, Santa Claus is coming to town again.

This year he almost didn't make it. His big heart was ailing, his spirits down.

But when he remembered "the joy that lights up kids' faces" every time he appears, he knew he couldn't let them down.

This is the 51st year that Steve Papa has put on his Santa suit. He lit the Christmas tree on the New Haven Green and he's making his usual rounds of schools and hospitals, spreading joy wherever he appears.

Three months ago, Papa lay in a hospital bed, recovering from open heart surgery.

"I was very depressed. I was thinking, 'Oh God, does this mean my Santa Claus days are over?'"

Even in the hospital the nurses called him "Santa." He played the part, wearing his red shirt and red hat with bells.

After his release from the hospital, Papa began physical therapy, attending the St. Raphael Hospital's "Take Heart" sessions in his red jogging suit.

His strength and confidence began to return; his beard grew back, long and fluffy.

But it's obvious the best therapy for Papa is being Santa. "This is my medicine," he said.

Papa does look remarkably like Santa, even out of uniform. During a recent conversation at his home on Chapel Street, Papa appeared to be feeling very chipper and raring to go.

"Maybe this was an early Christmas present, having a good recovery and knowing that I could be Santa Claus again. I thank God every day that he gives me the strength to continue it.

"It gets a little harder every year," said Papa, who is 70. "I don't want to tell the kids that Santa Claus is getting old. Santa doesn't get old. I want them to know Santa will always be there."

Even when he goes shopping or out for a walk, Papa wears his red hat with the jingling bells. The kids hear him coming. They cry out, "Look, Mommy! There's Santa Claus!" Others say, "Hey Santa—don't forget me! Christmas is coming soon!"

"When you see the joy on their faces, that's a feeling you can't get anywhere," Papa said.

Sometimes the kids tug his beard. Then they shout, "Mommy, he's real! He's the real one!" And Papa's heart soars.

"I almost feel like the real Santa Claus," he said. "I wish I could get in a sleigh and fly. This is what I should've been—the real one."

Papa isn't in this for the money. "A lady called and asked me to appear as Santa on upper State Street. She asked, 'What's the charge?' How could Santa charge money? That would take the fun out of it."

He also visits elderly patients in hospitals; those people are going through what he recently experienced. "It cheers them up tremendously. Everybody loves Santa Claus."

Papa has made one concession to surgery—he won't let the old gals sit on his lap.

Asked how the kids have changed during his 51 years as Santa, Papa said, "It used to be I could go to the fourth and fifth grades and they'd still believe. Today I don't usually go beyond the third grade.

"They weren't as demanding before. They'd ask for a wagon, a baseball glove, a Raggedy Ann doll, a new pair of boots. Now it's 'Santa, I want the "Star Wars" spaceship.' They want robots, ray guns, electronic games, computers."

Papa has worn out several Santa suits; his wife Helen keeps making new ones for him. And he goes to a beauty salon to have his beard curled just right.

"To me, Santa Claus is sacred. I'm going to go on as long as these legs can carry me. I was Santa for my children, then I was Santa for *their* children. That's a tremendous feeling.

"My dream is to be Santa Claus for my great-grandchildren."

17

Runner Recalls Yale Touchdown in Photo Mural

(May 26, 1988)

THE PHOTOGRAPH CAPTURES AN EXTRAORDINARY MOMENT: A YALE runner carrying the football crosses the goal line, his mouth open, breathless; a Princeton defender makes a desperate, futile lunge; a male Yale cheerleader leaps into the air; a sea of faces at the Yale Bowl goes wild with joy.

This scene covers almost an entire wall in the dining room at Kavanagh's on Chapel Street. A brass plate reads: "Denny McGill scores touchdown, November 17, 1956. Yale 42-Princeton 20."

For more than 30 years that photo mural has drawn the eyes of patrons, initially when the place was Jocko Sullivan's. When it was remodeled as Kavanagh's 10 years ago, the new owners had the good sense not to tamper with the big picture.

Where is Denny McGill today? Does he know he is immortalized on that wall, 32 years after he scored that touchdown?

After months of searching I finally tracked down Dennis L. McGill, attorney, 53 years old, now living in Jersey City, New Jersey.

He cannot believe the photograph is still up there. But he is very touched to hear it.

"Somebody asked me recently what had happened to it and I said, 'Gee, it'd be a pretty old shot to be up there after all these years.'"

McGill doesn't know who the photographer was. Frank Conte, Kavanagh's co-owner, said it was a Yale student (whose name Conte can't

The iconic photo of Denny McGill scoring that touchdown for Yale. (*Yale Daily News*)

recall) who was on assignment for the Yale Daily News and preserved the moment. Conte said the mystery photographer is now a doctor in Boston or New York.

With a little coaxing, McGill started to reminisce, the voice on the phone getting increasingly animated. "It's a vivid game in my mind. I remember scoring two touchdowns that day, both of which came off of passes. Dean Loucks was the quarterback.

"It was a key game; Princeton and we were tied for the Ivy League lead. The Bowl was packed with people (67,000—the largest crowd in years). We were ahead, 35-14 at halftime and it ended 42-20 as I recall. We wound up beating Harvard as well at Harvard Stadium. We were the Ivy League champs that year.

"The unique thing about that photo is the photographer was obviously in the end zone, looking back at the stands. He caught everybody's expressions; that made it outstanding.

"It's not just a ballplayer crossing the line—it's all the people involved. It captures all those emotions in that one shot.

"It's representative of the Yale mystique or spirit. That I happened to be in it was nice. It's a nice memory.

"I was very close to Jocko. He was like a second father to me. Somehow he got hold of that picture and made it into what I referred to as 'wallpaper.' I think that was in the following spring, my senior year. After Jocko passed away, his son kept it there.

"Jocko was like the Toots Shor of New Haven, a very personable guy. He took to me, I guess, because I was Irish and so was he.

"He came to the aid of a guy who was lonesome in kind of an overpowering university and town. He put me at ease, introduced me to a lot of people. He brought people from all walks of life together.

"He would call me up at eleven o'clock at night and say, 'Denny, what're you doing? You finished studying? Why don't you come over and have a sandwich?' He made the greatest roast beef sandwiches I can remember.

"When I graduated, I thought so much of him that I gave him a watch with an inscription on the back: 'Thanks for everything. To me, you've been like a second father.'

"He was buried with that watch."

McGill thinks he might have a copy of the famous photograph somewhere in his files. He hopes to come back to New Haven some day and take another look at the real thing.

18

Under Hard Shell Beats a Heart as Sweet as a Nut

(June 12, 1988)

"The Nut Lady," dressed in a long, flowing purple gown, ecstatically greets her latest visitors at the entrance to the world's only nut museum, right here in Old Lyme, Connecticut.

When her two guests, both young women, tell her this is their fourth visit, she gasps.

"I'm speechless! Have you seen me on 'Johnny Carson'?...You DID?"

Her real name is Elizabeth Tashjian but she is known the world over (she will tell you) as "the Nut Lady." She prefers to be called "the nut visionary."

"David Letterman coined that. I've been on his show three times. I got more applause than Smokey Robinson. I've been on 'Johnny Carson' four times and 'The Best of Johnny' twice. They put me in 'Ripley's Believe it or Not.'"

You think it's easy being "the Nut Lady"? You think it's all bright TV lights, big city?

Think again. "It's not easy putting nuts on the map," she confides wearily.

Nuts don't get much respect, nor does "the Nut Lady." She's just good fodder for a few minutes, a foil for Letterman or Carson to play with as the crowd yuks it up. She sadly admits she has been "exploited" by TV people.

Elizabeth Tashjian, "The Nut Lady," in her room at the Gladeview Health Care Center in Old Saybrook in 2002, shows off a 35-pound coco-de-mer nut she sculpted. (*New Haven Register* photographer Arnold Gold)

Then there are the omnipresent vandals who have stolen her nut museum signs, her four-feet-tall squirrel statue and her nut sculpture. Another nemesis: "The Connecticut Vacation Guide" people who no longer list the museum in their book because they say there are squirrels romping loose inside the Victorian gingerbread house.

"The town health officer decided it's perfectly natural for a country home to have squirrels," she says, digging out a newspaper clipping affirming this statement.

"I'm holding my head up," she says. "I'm here in 1988 after 16 years—sweet 16! I reclaimed my celebrity status by getting back on 'Johnny Carson' on December 3, 1987 and 'The Today Show' on October 26, 1987. Another person would have quit long ago. I have strong fortitude."

She appears to be in her 50s or 60s but she never divulges her age. "I am born anew every day!" she declares.

She tells her visitors, "This museum is a place where whimsy tries its wings and creativity flies. We should all be open to whimsy."

Her "tour" is really a rambling stream-of-consciousness rap about the beauty and value of nuts. She bubbles over in a kind of rhapsody while showing off her 10-feet-tall nutcracker ("here nuts and nutcrackers live in harmony"), her 35-pound coconut from the Seychelles Islands and modeling her nut masks ("This is King Cashew").

Another highlight is her spirited rendition of her very own "Nut Anthem." She spontaneously bursts into it in her high sing-song voice: "Nuts can be so bee-yoo-ti-full . . ."

"I consider nuts works of art," she says. (She's also an artist, a painter of—nuts). "Nuts are ideas, entities. Humanity evolved from the nut. Nuts are fresh tokens of primeval existence.

"From nuts we learn gentleness and respect. Nuts are hard outside, soft and sweet inside. I devour those sweet chestnuts!"

When she was a child, her parents kept plenty of bowls of nuts around. One day, in the midst of eating one, she saw its beauty and started painting them.

She lives alone but says, "You can never be lonely with nuts around. Just get a bowl and start cracking; you'll be cracking smiles."

She never drives a car, preferring to ride her bicycle around town. "I live a very Spartan life, to encourage the reception of ideas.

"I love my sweet solitude, I yearn for privacy. But I have to face the public, feed the requests, the visitors. Ah, it's a battle!"

19

Projectionist, Movie Crowd
Lose Best Friend

(August 18, 1988)

SIMCHA, THE BIG WHITE SAMOYED WITH THE BEAUTIFUL FLUFFY FUR and sensitive, communicative eyes, gave the York Square Cinemas a warmth and ambience.

Nobody, it seemed, could walk through the theater lobby without stopping to pat and stroke Simcha. She was the best-known and most beloved dog in New Haven.

But nobody loved her more than Arnold Gorlick, the York Square manager and projectionist, who brought her everywhere he went.

Simcha died last week.

At the age of 13, her legs finally gave out. And Gorlick had to make the toughest decision of his life. When he saw her pain and immobility, he knew what he had to do.

"What hurts so much is that I had to have her destroyed," said Gorlick, a bearded, animated and emotional man who wept several times during our cathartic interview.

"She just couldn't walk; she wouldn't ever walk again. She had arthritis in her spine and hips."

Gorlick sat on the carpet of the lobby—a place where he had spent countless hours playing with Simcha—and he reminisced about her, occasionally leaping to his feet to act out a story.

Arnold Gorlick and Simcha. (Photo by T. Charles Erickson)

"'Simcha' is Yiddish for joy, pleasure, happiness, a great occasion. When I got her I was engaged; she was part of our household. Then my engagement was broken but I was still living with Simcha.

"I couldn't leave her at home all day, so I would take her with me. She was welcomed in restaurants, doctors' offices, the barber shop . . . She aroused people because she was beautiful. But she also had a beautiful spirit. She made such eye contact."

Simcha debuted at the York Square in September, 1975. It would be a wildly successful 13-year run.

Her biggest crowd-pleaser was standing on her hind legs at the lobby's water fountain, hitting the button and quenching her thirst, a trick she learned herself.

"One percent of the people thought it was disgusting," Gorlick said. "Ninety-nine percent would stand in line behind her."

But that one percent caused problems. The York Square's insurance company received complaints and worried about liability. Gorlick, with the generous support of York Square owners Robert Spodick and

Leonard Sampson, negotiated a deal with the insurers: Simcha would stay beneath the lobby sofa-bench when the movies let out.

As a result, Gorlick often would walk into the lobby and see people on their hands and knees, under the bench, petting Simcha. (He got down under the bench and demonstrated.)

Simcha was considered part of the York Square staff. On Sundays the employees would order a Pepe's pizza; Simcha ate the crust. On her birthday she was treated to the whole pizza.

For various periods in the early 1980s, theatergoers were treated to the sight of "twin" Simchas; the other dog was her brother, Macbeth. Gorlick would sometimes "babysit" for Macbeth. He died last year of a heart attack.

"I wish Simcha could've gone like that," Gorlick said. "What made it so difficult was that the glow was still in her eyes."

Gorlick brought Simcha to Dr. Barbara Breu, who a year ago saved Simcha from bloat during an emergency operation. But Gorlick and Breu realized there could be no second "miracle cure."

"My uncle got Simcha a big scoop of ice cream—vanilla. That was her last act of pleasure.

"I stayed with her until her last breath; I held her in my arms. Even in death she looked beautiful."

Gorlick paused to compose himself. "Everywhere I go, people ask me, 'Where's the dog?' When I tell them, they start crying. She was like a person.

"I may ask that her ashes be buried with me. Because I'll never forget her. I miss her terribly."

20

Webb and Fred on the Edge of Being Broke

(September 25, 1988)

CHARLES WEBB AND HIS EX-WIFE FRED ARE LIVING THE LIFE ON THE edge that Benjamin Braddock and his beloved Elaine faced in the book Webb wrote: "The Graduate."

After giving away two houses and wandering from campground to campground in California for 10 years, Webb and Fred now find themselves at the Sea Gull Motel on Route 6 in Bethel. Their life savings: $440. Their material goods: a beat-up 1968 van that doesn't run.

But they have each other and their dog, Mrs. R.—named after Mrs. Robinson, the "Graduate" character immortalized in a song by Simon and Garfunkel.

They also have a plan: writing a sequel to "The Graduate," for which Fred, an artist, will do sketches. It will be set in the Bethel-Danbury area and tell what happens after that famous final scene in which Braddock busts up Elaine's wedding (to a rich snob) and escapes with her on a bus.

"Benjamin might wish he'd turn into a yuppie but he couldn't if he tried," Webb said. "Same with Elaine. They'd do odd jobs, whatever came along. To them, the paramount value is their relationship."

Webb and Fred drew a few looks when they walked into the Poseidon Diner across the street from the Sea Gull. Fred, 48, wore cowboy boots and a black cowboy hat with a red bandana tucked underneath. Webb, 49, looked relatively normal with his mustache and medium-length hair but he wore sandals and had an amused, ironic twinkle in his eyes.

He wrote "The Graduate" in 1962 after graduating from Williams College in Williamstown, Massachusetts. It became a hit movie in 1968. "For 20 years people have asked me, 'What happens next?' Besides, what has happened to us here must be told."

It does sound like the stuff of crazy fiction. In June, they came to New England so Webb could set up a fellowship at Williams, but no funds were available. Meanwhile, a newspaper there reported that the author of "The Graduate" was broke. The Associated Press picked up the story and suddenly Webb and Fred were national news.

Enter Marcelle Hall, 70, of Danbury, who read the article and felt sorry for them. She offered shelter and they gratefully accepted.

All was fine and dandy at the Hall house until Hall went away for a few days and read another newspaper article, this one reporting that the fun couple were hanging around in her home in the nude.

"We call it 'the Saturday night massacre,'" Webb said. "She told us, 'You people from the '60s never grow up!'"

Exit Webb and Fred and Mrs. R. They went on to several motels in Danbury and Bethel, the latest being the Sea Gull: $40 a night, bright orange doors.

"To call this a desperate situation would be kind of an understatement," Webb told another reporter over the phone as he sat on his bed at the Sea Gull.

Webb and Fred admit they feel "insecure" and a tad concerned about their future. But they have no regrets about giving away their possessions.

They lived in a house in Williamstown for four days, then bequeathed it to the Audubon Society. They lasted in the second one, a Spanish style bungalow in California, for two weeks. They gave that one to their real estate agent.

"We're just not into property," said Webb. "We get depressed in houses."

They got divorced because, Fred said, "The man is legally bound to support his wife. The wife is dependent, like a child."

Why does she call herself Fred? "I don't like to be associated with my real name, because I'm myself. I've always liked Freds."

They have two sons, both graduate students, who ask their parents: "Haven't you two run out of causes yet?"

Fred quotes the author of "On the Road," Jack Kerouac: "I'd rather be dead than be an adult."

21

Imperious Bart Was a "Simpler Creature" at Heart

(September 7, 1989)

THE LAST TIME I SAW A. BARTLETT GIAMATTI, HE WAS STANDING BY the newsstand in New Haven's Union Station, buying a paper—probably one carrying the latest sad news about the Boston Red Sox.

This was two years ago and, as usual, his beloved Sox were giving their fans a tough time. He appeared tired, disheveled and weighed down with his baggage and the baseball scores and his duties then as president of the National League. But, as I am a Yankee fan, I couldn't resist getting in a jab.

"I'm very sorry," I told him with mock sorrow. "It just isn't their year."

He chuckled, tucked the paper under his arm and shuffled off toward the train.

I remember thinking at the time that he looked terrible. The same thought occurred to me two weeks ago when I watched him on TV as he announced he was banning Pete Rose from baseball. Giamatti's face was haggard. I was shocked by how old he seemed. He was only 51; he looked at least 60.

And so when my father—a longtime Red Sox fan—called me last Friday and told me that Bart Giamatti had dropped dead from a heart attack, I was saddened but maybe not so surprised.

I have been reading all the tributes to him, but with a jaded eye. Unlike most New Haveners and baseball fans, I didn't really like the guy. I respected him—especially for the way he handled Rose—but I found him to be a tad imperious and highfalutin.

I developed this prejudice in 1981 to 1982 while I was covering Yale for the *Register* and Giamatti was Yale's president. During that time I was able to meet Giamatti only once, at a "tea" where he mingled with students. He was charming, personable and eloquent. But I always had problems getting him to return my phone calls for comments on news stories. Sometimes I would find his answers to my questions in the *New York Times.*

Yale University President A. Bartlett Giamatti. (*New Haven Register* file photo)

However, over the past year, while writing about Yale's old institutions for the Yale Alumni Magazine, I repeatedly encountered small businessmen who simply loved Bart Giamatti.

I heard this from Rocky D'Eugenio of Phil's Hair Styles on Wall Street, who for many years cut Giamatti's hair; from Manson Whitlock of the Whitlock Typewriter Shop, who sold Giamatti a Smith-Corona; from Lewis Beckwith, who served Giamatti countless cheeseburgers at the Yankee Doodle Coffee Shop; and from Elliot Brause of Quality Liquor Store. All of them said: He was a nice guy. He always came back and saw us. He was unfailingly friendly.

Giamatti also scored runs in my book for being a baseball purist. He loathed modern technological scoreboards which distract from the game and he had a healthy hatred for artificial grass and the designated hitter. He loved the old ball parks, with their organ music and real grass.

He wrote about this beautifully. I looked up his essay "The Green Fields of the Mind," reprinted in the anthology "Baseball, I Gave You All the Best Years of My Life." In that piece, he described the heartbreak of sitting in Fenway Park on the last day of the regular season in 1977, when the Red Sox once again came close but failed to win the pennant. The season was over.

"Of course there are those who learn after the first few times," Giamatti wrote. "They grow out of sports. And there are others who were born with the wisdom to know that nothing lasts. These are the truly tough among us, the ones who can live without illusion, or without even the hope of illusion.

"I am not that grown-up or up-to-date. I am a simpler creature, tied to more primitive patterns and cycles. I need to think something lasts forever, and it might as well be that state of being that is a game; it might as well be that, in a green field, in the sun."

Rest there in peace.

22

Spanky Delights College Crowd With Gang's Tales

(September 24, 1989)

THERE HE WAS—SPANKY!—STANDING UNNOTICED AMID THE CROWD IN the cafeteria at Southern Connecticut State University, college kids towering over him.

Everybody's eyes were riveted to the screen, fixed on the image of a cute little kid in top hat and cane: the Spanky of "Our Gang," more than 50 years ago.

Today's Spanky McFarland, dressed in a blue suit and red tie, glasses, gray hair—slightly balding—is still chubby, which is not so cute at age 61.

But he also has a big heart. During his appearance Thursday he thoroughly charmed the standing-room-only crowd of students.

After they had been treated to clips from Spanky's career, the man walked out of the crowd, stepped up onto the stage and began, in his Texas drawl, to tell wonderful stories about those golden years.

The "Our Gang" or "Little Rascals" series began in 1922, six years before Spanky (George Robert Phillips McFarland) was born. Producer Hal Roach assembled the cutest, most natural crop of kids he could find and turned them loose in front of a camera.

There were 221 episodes; Spanky appeared in 95 of them. The last one was made in 1944. After a successful run in movie theaters, the "Gang" was discovered by new generations on TV, beginning in the 1950s. That discovery continues among the kids of today.

"I was born in Dallas," Spanky said. "I modeled baby clothes when I was two-to-three years old. After I did an ad for Wonder Bread, I got a screen test with Hal Roach. And the fat kid got lucky.

"I started with 'Our Gang' when I was three and stayed 'til I was 16 (1931-1944). How did I get to be the leader of the 'Gang'? I outlasted everybody. The only way I grew was this way (he spread his hands). I stayed short."

Spanky then showed slides of his old "Gang" members and told their stories.

Stymie (Matthew Beard): "Stymie was my best friend. He took me under his wing. Unfortunately, in later years, Stymie got into heroin and did time in prison. Then he got cleaned up and worked in TV again. We finally resumed our friendship. In 1980, he had a stroke and died. I will miss him until the day I die."

Darla (Darla Hood): "She went on to become the first voice of the 'Chicken of the Sea' mermaid. Her singing career never went anywhere and I don't understand that. Darla died of a heart attack in 1979 when she was only 47. The whole 'Gang' missed her."

Alfalfa (Carl Switzer): "Arbitrarily the most popular member of the 'Gang'—next to me! He was good—but he *could not sing*, folks. This kid could not carry a tune in a bucket!

"Alfalfa was mischievous and that may have led to his early demise, in 1959 (at age 31). His partner in a hunting business had lost a dog and offered a $50 reward. When Alfalfa found the dog, he wanted the $50. He and his partner got into an argument, Alfalfa pulled a knife on him and the guy shot him. Alfalfa didn't have a good knowledge of right and wrong; it cost him his life."

Spanky got angry while discussing Buckwheat (William Henry Thomas Jr.) "There was a gentleman on 'Saturday Night Live' (Eddie Murphy) who portrayed Buckwheat. I thought it was in poor taste. I thought it was tacky. An awful thing to do. And Buckwheat never said 'O-tay.' Porky (Eugene Gordon Lee) said that.

"Buckwheat wasn't around to defend himself—he died of a heart attack in 1981. I miss him and I hope you all do too."

Spanky said he never got any residual payments for "Our Gang." "My residual is the interest, hopefully the love and attention that you all gave me when you came to see the little fat man tell about what he did 50 years ago.

"I'm probably one of the luckiest guys in the world. I have nothing but good memories of my career and of my return to normal life in 1944." (He did sales work for Philco-Ford in Texas).

"I am blessed. I guess I've been blessed since I was born."

23

Another City Fixture Fades into History

(October 31, 1999)

THE SIGN ON THE FRONT DOOR OF ELLIOT BRAUSE'S QUALITY WINE Shop is like a symbolic tombstone for what's happening to more and more longtime mom and pop shops in this old town.

It reads: "We have lost our lease. So after 65 years and four generations, on October 30 we will close our doors forever. Thanks for your loyal patronage. Goodbye, God bless—Elliot, David and B.J."

David is Elliot's son, who ran the shop with him and had hoped to stay there many more years. Instead David had to go out and get another job, working for a wine wholesaler.

B.J. is Elliot's dog, a Cardigan Welch Corgi who was sitting in his usual spot by the front door Friday, the next-to-last day of business.

B.J., the third generation of Corgis who have greeted customers, represents the personal, eccentric touch which we are losing amid the drive for sameness and big names.

B.J. must have wondered what was going on as droves of old friends came into the store one last time to say good-bye.

"He'll miss this block more than any of us," Brause said. "He hates Sundays. He's here with us six days a week."

The Brauses lost their lease because, like another longtime business, Broadway Pizza, they were in the way of Yale's plans to redevelop Broadway.

Yale's master plan is to tear down several Broadway storefronts and replace them with bigger buildings for bigger retail outfits.

For months, Brause negotiated with Yale about moving him around the corner on York Street.

Brause sought a 10-year lease. He said Yale told him, "We don't do that. Five years only."

"I need long-term planning," Brause said. "Yale wouldn't give me that."

Yale spokesmen say they regret Brause's departure and insist they went "the extra mile" in trying to work out a deal.

Yale officials also say they will offer a balance of mom-and-pop businesses and national chain stores. But this "balance" is becoming an out of kilter see-saw with one big fat rider.

"They're making this nice little block into a strip mall and putting the little guys around the corner," Brause said. "They're doing irreparable damage here."

Brause has mixed emotions about Yale because it has been his "bread and butter." And it has "a lot of pieces," some wonderful, some quite the opposite.

"Yale has many good, hard-working people who care for this community," he said. "And then there are the little fiefdoms. They profess to have a sense of community, tradition and loyalty—and they have none of those."

Jimmy Dixon, who worked for 50 years at the Yale Co-Op on Broadway before Yale kicked out that store and brought in Barnes & Noble, came in and hugged Brause.

"I would never come to New Haven except for you," Dixon said.

"Now we're just another piece of history," Brause replied.

The family history began when his grandfather, Harry Rosenfeld, came here from Russia in the late 1800s and worked as a fruit peddler pushing a cart.

That cart led to a Broadway grocery and, in 1934, to the wine shop. Elliot's father, Harold Brause, ran the wine shop until he died in the early 1960s.

Elliot, 62, has run the place ever since.

"I love this city and being here," said Brause, still a New Haven resident. "I'll miss it terribly."

And the people of New Haven will miss Elliot, David and B.J. terribly.

24

Yogi the Cat Gave Family 14 Great Years

(April 16, 2000)

THE FIRST TIME I EVER SAW YOGI, HE WAS SITTING IN A CAGE, LOOKING out at me, his green eyes expectant.

I was not a "cat person," as I had repeatedly told my wife. I was raised in a family that treasured dogs. Cats were "aloof." You couldn't connect with them.

But when the attendant opened the cage at the Hartford animal shelter and I held that small ball of yellow fur, he started purring lustily and poked his little nose into my armpit.

Never again did he have to live in a cage.

We named him after Yogi Berra. My wife figured this might make her Yankee fan husband more receptive.

"Don't worry," she told me that first night. "He'll just sleep at the foot of the bed."

When I woke up the next morning, Yogi was curled up against my head, nestled on my pillow, purring in ecstasy.

And for the 14 years that followed, he stayed there with us, always purring as if he still couldn't believe his good fortune. If my wife or I awoke in the middle of the night with worries or if one of us was sick, he would be beside us, reassuring with that beautiful blissful sound.

When we moved back to New Haven, bought a house and had our first child, Yogi was an avid participant. We were concerned he'd be jealous because he didn't get as much lap time with "Dad." But he loved our Natalie and curled up with her too.

Yogi with co-owner Jennifer Kaylin. (Photo by Randall Beach)

Natalie's first word was "Gogi."

Two years later, our second daughter Charlotte's first word was "Gogi" too.

Yogi never got sick, was always spry and happy. And so three weeks ago, when we woke up in the morning and he was not on our pillow but was downstairs on the couch by himself, we knew something was terribly wrong.

The doctors in New Haven thought they saw "blockage" in Yogi's throat on the X-ray. They recommended I take him immediately to a specialist in Norwalk.

During our drive down there, he didn't want to sit on my lap anymore; he just crouched on the back seat in a pained daze.

"Hang on, Yogi," I told him. "You can beat this."

After I carried him into the receiving room, the doctors looked at the X-ray and concluded Yogi had cancer. It had spread from his throat into his lungs.

The chief doctor, with a slight catch in his voice, recommended Yogi be "put to sleep."

Stunned, I called my wife. We reluctantly agreed that since Yogi had given us so much, the least we could do in return was give him relief from his suffering.

Yogi had always been there for me, so I resolved to be there for him at the end.

I went into a small room with a chrome table and stroked "my boy" as the doctor prepared the needle. I whispered into Yogi's ear, "Thanks, boy."

Then I took a breath, nodded to the doctor and he made the ejection.

The poison shot instantly into Yogi's gentle heart. He dropped into my arms and was at peace.

It was a long, solitary, teary-eyed drive back to New Haven. Then we had to tell our two girls, in an agonizing emotional scene in our kitchen, that Yogi was gone.

Our house has never felt so empty.

But he taught us so much in 14 great, ever-giving years.

Thanks, Yogi.

25

A Father's Legacy Keeps the Yankee Doodle Coffee Shop Sizzling

(September 22, 2002)

WHEN ANOTHER SATISFIED CUSTOMER ROSE FROM ONE OF THE 12 TUR-quoise stools at the Yankee Doodle Coffee Shop, he stopped by the door to speak with the man at the grill, Rick Beckwith.

"I don't come in here very often," said the customer, who was dressed in the uniform of a blue-collar worker. "But I remember your dad. I just wanted to say I'm sorry for your loss . . . Carry on."

Beckwith treasures such moments. He loves hearing people talk about his dad, Lewis Beckwith Jr. But two months later, it still hurts.

"It's difficult," he said. "Every day there are more cards, emails, people coming in and talking about him. Just being here is a constant reminder. Everywhere I look, I see my father."

And yet Beckwith, 39, and his sister, Darlene Richetelli, 37, do carry on at the grill and counter of this Elm Street institution adjacent to the Yale campus.

They do it because of the legacy of their father and of their grand-father, Lewis Beckwith Sr., who opened the Doodle in 1950. They do it because their father always told them, "All things come from work."

When he finally retired in 2000 after celebrating the Doodle's 50th birthday, Beckwith Jr. was looking forward to enjoying something new: leisure time. But only a few months later he was diagnosed with bone cancer.

On July 18, he lost his 18-month battle. He was 64.

"He died on a Thursday, Beckwith said. "We opened the following Monday. That's what he would've wanted."

For any of us complaining about our work hours, consider what Beckwith does: every Monday through Saturday he gets up at 3:30 a.m. By 4:15 a.m., he's at his place by the grill, getting ready.

At 5 a.m. he calls his sister.

"My father used to call me every morning to wake me up," she said. "Now my brother does it. It's my alarm clock."

She reaches the Doodle by 5:45 a.m. At 6 a.m. they open the door for customers.

Beckwith remains at his post until 7:30 p.m., closing time.

For extra help, his mother, Pat Beckwith, comes in several days a week.

During our morning talk by the grill, the phone rang. Beckwith answered, listened carefully, then turned to his sister and said quietly, "She broke her arm."

He explained to me that his mom fell in her home a few weeks ago. She thought it was just a bruise but finally she saw a doctor.

Beckwith predicted she would come to work the next day. "We're used to working sick. It's one thing our dad instilled in us: you get out of bed in the morning."

Yes, and you hold onto the great traditions, such as the Doodle Hamburger Hall of Fame.

The winners are listed on a gold plaque by the door: those immortal carnivores who have consumed the most hamburgers in one sitting.

The current record-holder, and it has stood for three years, is William Stobierski of Ansonia, who put away 28 burgers. You might have seen him on Fox TV's "The Glutton Bowl."

But now there is a challenger. A Yale worker named Clarence has vowed to come in and eat at least 29.

Lewis Beckwith Jr. also liked his burgers. The Doodle advertises "Lew's Special: two double cheeseburgers plus one large vanilla coke—$8.95."

"Every Friday after he finished work," Rick Beckwith said, "my dad would sit down and eat that meal.

"So many things have changed," he said as he looked out the window at the new upscale shops on Broadway. "We keep everything the way it is; that's the way our customers like it. It feels like home to them."

Beckwith added, "Our family wants to thank the community for all the support we've received. We never realized how many people my father and the Doodle have touched."

Asked what the people have been saying about his father, Beckwith replied, "What a great man he was . . . Classy . . . A hard worker."

26

Vonnegut Has Sharp Words for President, War and Censorship

(May 2, 2003)

WHEN KURT VONNEGUT ARRIVED AT THE MARK TWAIN HOUSE IN Hartford Wednesday afternoon, three of his awestruck fans (including me) were sitting on the old porch in sweaty anticipation.

"I can't believe it!" said Jim Hostetler of Middletown, who was there with his wife, Sandy. "This is the equivalent of meeting (Rolling Stones guitarist) Keith Richards!"

No, it was even better than that.

Here was one of America's greatest 20th century writer-satirists, coming to tour the homestead of the country's greatest 19th century writer-satirist.

But this wasn't just a tourist jaunt for Vonnegut, author of "Slaughterhouse-Five," "Cat's Cradle" and many other novels.

He's mad as hell at President George W. Bush for the war in Iraq and cutting social programs. He had plenty to say about that on Wednesday night during a speech at the Hartford Financial Service Group to a packed audience.

Vonnegut is 80 now but he rarely seemed tired during his house tour, a cocktail reception and hour-long lecture.

After he emerged from a limousine with his wife, the photographer Jill Krementz, and their 20-year-old daughter Lily, he wanted to be left alone to smoke cigarettes on a corner of the porch.

Kurt Vonnegut at the Mark Twain House in Hartford. (*New Haven Register* photographer Mara Lavitt)

But eventually I was permitted to take a seat next to the great man and ask him a few questions.

I mentioned the New Haven Board of Aldermen that night would hold a public hearing on a proposed resolution asking people not to use the word "nigger."

This term was used frequently in Twain's "Adventures of Huckleberry Finn," a portrait of a friendship between a white boy, Huck, and Jim, a black runaway slave. Vonnegut Wednesday night would call that book "the greatest of all American novels."

Vonnegut told me he agreed the word is offensive in most contexts. But he said government officials have no business advising people what they can or cannot say.

"People should be able to use all words," he said, then smiled and unleashed a few unprintable examples.

When I asked him about the war in Iraq, he shook his head and sighed. This is a man who fought at the Battle of the Bulge in World War II and survived the allied bombing of Dresden, Germany as a prisoner of war.

"We hate war," he said of his generation. "And this one (Iraq) was undertaken so casually . . ."

Later, during the tour of Twain's home, Vonnegut remained irreverent, even though he has described the place as "sacred."

Gazing at some of the elaborate fixtures, he said, "So vulgar!" Then he smiled and asked, "Am I the first person to say that?"

Vonnegut was more impressed when we got upstairs, into the billiards room where Twain shot pool and wrote "Huckleberry Finn," among other works.

After hearing these details from the tour guide, Vonnegut said, "I have a question. My daughter Lily is a pool shark. Can she shoot a game?"

But John Boyer, executive director of the Mark Twain House, said he would "have to take that up with the board."

His spirits undiminished by this setback, Vonnegut remarked as he exited, "I like that room, I tell you!"

That evening Vonnegut made many direct hits on Bush.

"Arabs are so 'dumb,' they invented algebra," Vonnegut said. "I thought George W. Bush hated Arabs so much on account of algebra. But I don't think he knows that much history."

Vonnegut derided the U.S. military term "shock and awe." He said, "It can be compressed into one word: murder."

During the questions session, a man asked Vonnegut, "Does anything give you hope?"

Vonnegut was silent for a moment. Then he replied, "Uh . . . I'm going to have a drink after this."

27

The Late Great Kavanagh's, Where Even Red Sox Fans Were Welcome

(July 6, 2003)

THERE WAS NO OTHER PLACE QUITE LIKE KAVANAGH'S.

It is painful to be using the past tense, but my favorite bar-restaurant and gathering spot has gone out of business.

This Chapel Street hangout was visited by celebrities such as Paul Newman and Bruce Springsteen. But it was the regulars, the colorful mix of townies and Yalies, that made Kavanagh's so special.

I had no chance to say goodbye. A few of the regulars had a final night there in May, then unceremoniously closed the doors.

Not even Mike Kavanagh himself was there that night.

Kavanagh, who co-owned the establishment with Frank Conte, stayed back at his home off Townsend Avenue.

Kavanagh used to be a fixture at his namesake, tending the bar or sitting on the other side of it, buying drinks for customers and telling stories.

But two years ago he suffered a stroke. He moves around now with the aid of a cane.

"I didn't want to be there the last night," he said as he sat in his living room. "It'd be kind of sad."

Kavanagh said he knew the place couldn't survive for long after his partner died. Frank Conte died on April 23.

A sign in the front window at 1166 Chapel Street says "Closed for renovations." But Kavanagh said the sign is misleading. The business is for sale.

He has brought much of the old place into his home. The Kavanagh's front lettering is now in his dining room. The wonderful wooden phone booth that stood in the corner by the bar now sits in his living room.

The giant Louisville Slugger baseball bat hangs in his front hallway. The pictures of fabled New York Yankees (Roger Maris, Babe Ruth, Lou Gehrig, Joe DiMaggio) and team photos of Yale athletes adorn the walls.

One prominent feature from Kavanagh's is still there: the sweeping black-and-white photograph of Yale halfback Denny McGill scoring a touchdown during the 1956 victory over Princeton at the Yale Bowl.

"It's part of the place; it's like wallpaper, so it can't be removed," Kavanagh said. "It was there back in Jocko's time."

Indeed, before Kavanagh's opened 25 years ago, that space was known as Jocko Sullivan's, another great sports bar where you could also hear live performances from folk singers such as Tom Paxton and Dave Van Ronk.

When Kavanagh and Conte opened up a quarter of a century ago, Kavanagh said, "I just wanted it to be comfortable for everybody, so anybody could come in. I never looked down my nose at anybody."

Kavanagh's longtime friend, Fred Sgro, said the idea was "to have a place where you could eat a cheeseburger, drink a beer and watch the Yankees."

Yankees fans like me loved this. We pinstripe loyalists always headed there for the big games in October.

"Our first year (1978), the Yankees were in the playoff game with the Red Sox," Kavanagh recalled. "I was behind the bar when Bucky Dent hit the home run (that helped win the American League title for the Yankees). That was a good way to kick things off. The place was packed."

Kavanagh has a much less happy memory of another Yankee game, in the October 2001 World Series.

"In game four or five, when the Yankees came back and beat Arizona, I spilled a drink. Then I spilled another one. I thought, 'This isn't like me. Something's wrong here.'"

It was the beginning of his stroke. He watched the rest of the Series in the hospital, including that awful seventh game. The rest of us regulars witnessed the shocking Yankees ninth-inning loss at Kavanagh's.

Kavanagh remembers other big nights there, such as the time actress Kathleen Turner strode in with Springsteen. The rock star sat nonchalantly at the bar, drinking light beers.

And then there was the Sunday morning Harry Belafonte was using that phone booth, angering the regulars who needed the phone to place football bets.

"Get out of there!" they told the famous singer. "We need that phone!" The singer obliged with a smile.

28

Ding! Ding! Ding! Here Comes the Retired Insurance Executive!

(August 17, 2003)

LIFE IN MADISON WASN'T AS SUNNY AND TASTY AND FUN 12 YEARS AGO as it is today.

Why? Joe Barbato was selling insurance instead of Good Humor ice cream.

"I had my own insurance business for 28 years," Barbato said, shaking his head as he thought about it.

"I got fed up with the corporate stuff, arguing with the company," he said.

And so Barbato retired, but still he was neither happy nor fulfilled. People around him weren't happy either.

Then one day in August 1991, his daughter saw an ad in the newspaper: "Good Humor Man wanted."

"I told her, 'I can't do that; there's no way,'" he recalled. "She said, 'Try it. You're driving us crazy.'"

Barbato, now 72, broke into a wide smile as he finished the story of how he became "Papa Joe."

"It's the best thing I ever did."

The second best thing he ever did was to bring his dog with him.

"Margaret was four months old when I started," he said. "I didn't want to leave her at home, so I just decided to take her with me."

"Papa Joe" Barbato on the Madison Green. (*New Haven Register* photographer Peter Hvizdak)

Barbato remembered that when he drove down Main Street, people would call out, "Hey Margaret! How ya doin'?"

"Margaret didn't know she was a dog," he said. "She thought she was a person. She looked at you as if she knew exactly what you were saying."

But three years ago Margaret developed cancer.

"She got a tumor on her cheek the size of a golf ball," Barbato said. "It was inoperable."

He turned to his classic Good Humor truck (few of which remain) and pointed to the inscription: "Painted by George and John of Madison Auto Body for Margaret."

"They painted this truck for me, for free, in her honor," he said.

After Margaret died, Barbato adopted Belle, a golden retriever with a sweet disposition and a sweet tooth.

Belle, now 10, sits in the truck above a sign that says: "Hi, my name is Belle. Try the toasted almond. It's delicious."

"She knows which one is the toasted almond," Barbato insisted. "She zeroes in on it."

"I give her two of them a day," he said, "and she steals three a day."

"The kids cry, 'Mommy, Mommy, the dog ate my ice cream!'" Barbato said. "I teach them to hold their ice cream out, away from her, and then they can pet her."

He said out-of-towners always ask if Belle might fall out of the truck.

"I trained her never to leave this truck," he said. "She won't even budge for a squirrel. If she sees another dog, she just turns up her nose."

Caryn Block, who stopped on the Madison Green to buy an ice cream for her son, Jacob Pfeifer, said Barbato is "amazing."

"He knows what flavor every kid likes," she said. "He has a personal relationship with each child."

That's why Barbato describes his job as "fun."

"I love kids, I'm out in the fresh air and I'm with my dog," he said. "I've got the best job in the world."

He admits his sales drop during rainy or humid weather, when people stay inside. And he said that because his job is seasonal, he relies on Social Security payments to supplement his income.

"In summertime I work seven days a week," he said. "If I don't make my usual run, people ask, 'Where were you? We waited.'

"The kids, you just can't imagine how big their eyes get," he said. "And that makes it all worthwhile."

Grown-ups love it, too, when they hear his bells ringing. He does parties and weddings, and he reported the Good Humor truck "brings back their youth."

It's much quieter at his Madison home. "My wife (Nancy) passed on 12 years ago," he said. "It's just Belle and me."

Before I said goodbye to "Papa Joe," I sampled one of his toasted almond bars. As I began to eat it, I noticed Belle was watching me intently, licking her chops.

I relented and she finished it off, licking the stick clean. Another satisfied customer.

29

Red Sox Fan Gets Punched in the Gut. Over and Over and Over . . .

(October 5, 2003)

WHEN I CALLED UP LEO VIGUE, THE LONG-SUFFERING, LONG-SERVING bartender at Rudy's bar and told him I wanted to celebrate the 25th anniversary of Bucky Dent's homer with him, he didn't get it.

"Why would you want to celebrate that?" he asked. "That was the worst day of my life!"

"But Leo, I'm very sentimental; I was at Rudy's that day," I said. "And I'm a Yankees fan."

I could hear him groaning into the phone. It was the kind of a deep, sorrowful sound only a fan of the Boston Red Sox can make.

I had hit on the idea of coming down to see Vigue when I realized that last Thursday (October 2) would be the 25th anniversary of a date that still lives in infamy for Red Sox fans.

They couldn't believe the sight of Dent's long fly ball vanishing over the top of "the Green Monster" at Boston's Fenway Park. Dent was the Yanks' light-hitting shortstop, so it was a particularly cruel blow in a cruel history.

Dent's three-run homer was the big moment in the Yanks' come-from-behind victory as they beat the Sox, 5-4, in a one-game playoff for the American League Championship.

"Happy anniversary, Leo!" I called out as I entered Rudy's, a fixture on the corner of Elm and Howe Streets.

Leo Vigue at Rudy's. (*New Haven Register* photographer Peter Hvizdak)

I was wearing my Yankees hat because I knew he would be wearing his Red Sox hat.

I was also carrying my *New Haven Register* story from October 3, 1978. The headline: "Sox Sympathizers Sob as Yank Rooters Roar." Beneath it was a photo of Vigue at the bar in his Sox hat.

Now, 25 years later, it was déjà vu all over again. Vigue had been up until 2:30 a.m., watching at his home as his Sox lost a division series game in the 12th inning to the Oakland Athletics.

"The Red Sox should pay us for the pain and aggravation we go through," he said. "We should sue them."

Meanwhile, his pain and suffering were about to be renewed: the Red Sox were starting another game. Vigue was watching it on the TV over the bar, as he did when Dent hit that homer.

"The place was packed that day," he recalled after a little coaxing. "I'd gone out and gotten champagne. When we lost, I refused to drink it."

"Now," he added, "we're suffering again. Why did they put that pitcher (Byung-Hyun Kim) in there in the ninth inning last night? I said, 'Oh no, we're going to blow it again.'"

When a customer asked Vigue if he believed in "the curse of the Bambino," that the Sox have not won a World Series since 1918 because the Sox sold Babe Ruth to the Yankees, Vigue snorted.

"That's crap," he said. "Hey, they had their chances and they blew it. Like Bucky Dent—there was no reason for them to blow that."

Naturally I brought up Bill Buckner, the infamous Sox first baseman who let a ground ball roll through his legs in that World Series game against the New York Mets in 1986.

"I wasn't here for that," Vigue said. "I watched it in Maine with my brother. He was very sick."

Then Vigue told me quietly that his brother died that night, shortly after the game ended. "He had predicted we were going to lose that game."

Vigue took time out to walk outside and show me the house he lives in around the corner from Rudy's. In front of it is a flagpole with a Red Sox flag.

"See, buddy, I've got my flag flying," he said. (He calls everybody "buddy.")

"Do you know what somebody did to me?" he added. "They took mine down and put up a Yankees flag! I was going to burn it, right in front of Rudy's."

Vigue, who is 69, said he has lived in that house for about 30 years and has tended bar at Rudy's for at least 35 years.

More customers were starting to come into Rudy's by 5 p.m. Friday. Many sang out, "Hey Leo, what happened last night?"

But he was preoccupied with watching the latest debacle. Aided by a wild throw, the Athletics were surging ahead, 5-0. The Sox would lose again.

"Oh God, this is terrible," Vigue said. "Unbelievable."

One of the regular customers, Mark Haney, looked at Vigue and remarked, "It's not easy being Leo."

30

A Job With Strings, a Life Without

(January 11, 2004)

JIMMY WEIL PACED AROUND THE ROOM, A GROWLING LION IN WINTER.

Weil is the longtime puppeteer at the Stony Creek Puppet House. He has no family nearby but the Sicilian puppets are his old friends and companions.

Now he is at a crossroads. The community threw a 60th birthday party for him Saturday at the Puppet House but he is not embracing his new decade.

"I'm 60 and I have gout in my legs," he said. "I'm too fat . . . I'm trying to figure out what to do with the rest of my life."

It's been quite a ride so far. His parents, Leonard Dankmar Weil and Grace Weil, adopted him upon his birth in New York City. They had lost their son Danke, who died after their boat blew up and burned at the Stony Creek dock.

"My parents were eccentric hippies," Weil said. "They were very sweet and loving. But they were frustrated by my problems."

Alternately sitting and getting up to fetch coffee or anything else that caught his eye, Weil said, "I have attention deficit disorder, trouble concentrating. My parents were intellectual and not manual. I'm the other way around."

He loved traveling around the world with his parents when he was young. The downside was going to nine schools until he dropped out after 10th grade.

Jimmy Weil. (*New Haven Register* photographer Peter Hvizdak)

"I had a fantastic childhood until I was shipped off to prep school," he said. "That began my depression.

"Other guys went to college," he said. "I went to therapy.

"Depression is only your negative head," he added. "Let's face it—being a human being isn't easy. It's complicated. Especially when you're 60."

Mulling over his next move, Weil looks back on his past jobs: a fisherman in Key West, a lumberman in Massachusetts, a banjo player all over, and a cab driver in New York.

But it's always been about the puppets, ever since he met Salvatore Macri in Sicily when Weil was five. Macri's dad did puppet shows there.

Weil's mom, a puppet collector, bought the exquisite puppets and had them shipped to America. In 1960, needing a place to display her collection for a planned puppet museum, she bought the little theater in Stony Creek.

Salvatore Macri eventually came to America and taught Weil how to be a puppeteer. This can take years.

Weil jumped up and grabbed one of the puppets. They are beautifully painted and about four feet tall, with distinctive faces and costumes.

"This guy is totally obnoxious," Weil said, moving the figure so he kicked me, hard, in my shin. "He's frustrated, angry.

"The great thing about puppets," Weil said, "is you can express the emotions you don't allow yourself to express. You have to be them; you can say anything you want."

Weil brought me backstage where the puppets were lined up, waiting for action.

"They're mad now because they're just hanging there," he said. "They need us to move them. They have a lot to say."

Weil looked wistfully at his old buddies. "We're trying to figure out what to do with them and the theater after I die. Should we donate them to the Smithsonian or keep on going here? I want them to keep moving; that's what they do."

Weil doesn't talk about one subject: his problems with Macri. They went to court over ownership of some of the puppets. Now it's in mediation.

Sometimes Weil thinks about going back to Florida, where he still has a boat. "I want to sail the Caribbean, but I can't seem to get down there. I want to sail; I'm not sure I'm strong enough."

Weil said, "I've been doing the puppets so long, I'm tired of it. But I also feel it's important. The puppets have been my responsibility all my life."

More shows area coming up January 17-18 and January 24-25. The play is Paul Hammer's "Give Me Back Jerusalem! It's Mine! No, It's Mine!" It's got lots of fights.

After that, who knows what's next for Weil and his theater and the puppets?

"It's a church without a steeple, it's for the people," he said. "I'd like to ask the town: What do they want?"

31

Forest Theater Goes Out With Fond Memories, Teary Eyes

(February 27, 2004)

MOST OF THE PEOPLE WHO WENT TO THE FOREST THEATER WEDNES-
day night, on its next-to-last day of operation, had already heard the sad
news.

For those who did not, a simple message posted on the old ticket
booth sufficed. It thanked customers for their patronage and said the staff
regretted this decision.

The sign ended: "We will close with a lot of great memories and continued friendships."

Inside, Richard Mallette Jr. and two longtime assistants were selling
a couple dozen tickets and a few bins of popcorn, running the upstairs
projector and reminiscing with sad-eyed customers.

This is how it ends for single-screen neighborhood movie theaters,
which one by one have vanished from our area. They won't be coming
back.

When Mallette called me last Friday afternoon, I knew immediately
what he was going to say. Many of us have watched the Forest slowly,
inexorably go from being a popular movie place to a quiet relic.

After my Forest news story ran in Saturday's Register, about 100
people came out to the theater that night to pay their respects and com-
miserate with Mallette.

"Somebody brought me a dozen roses," he said. "I'd never gotten flowers in my life!

"People are trying to talk me into staying open," Mallette added. "But they understand the situation."

"The situation" is not just declining attendance for small family-run movie houses.

Mallette is only 37 but he is ill. He can't continue to put in the long hours of building maintenance, movie bookings and ticket selling.

His doctors think his dizzy spells, numbness and double vision could mean he has multiple sclerosis. Soon he will travel to Germany for special treatment.

But he didn't want to close the family theater. His grandfather, Tony Terrazano, bought the place in the Allingtown neighborhood of West Haven around 1940 when it was only a couple of years old. Mallette helped out there as a teenager and gradually took over at the helm as his grandfather and grandmother, Irene, grew older.

Some of the old-time customers Wednesday night recalled how Mallette's grandfather walked up and down the aisles, stooping over and over again to pick up the candy wrappers.

But after the Terrazanos died and Mallette got sick, the end of the Forest was inevitable.

"Richie, you gave and gave and gave," his old neighbor Lori Moran told him Wednesday night. "Your grandfather is proud of you."

Moran recalled how she and "Richie," when they were kids, used to walk down the hill from their family homes to the Forest. They now live in other parts of West Haven.

"You've got to concentrate on your health, Richie," Moran said, endorsing his decision to close the theater and try to sell the building.

Mike, who declined to give his last name, stood behind the concessions stand with Mallette, recalling how he, too, grew up with him. Mike started coming to the Forest when he was one year old.

Around the corner, about 25 people were sitting in the faded blue seats, watching the early show of the comedy "Love Don't Cost a Thing." Senior citizens and kids had paid $3.50, adults $4.

When the movie ended, they drifted slowly into the lobby to see Mallette. Most of them simply said "good luck" and departed.

Robert Ford lingered to shake Mallette's hand and thank him.

"It's a part of history," Ford said. "I just wanted to be here."

"Going to the movies will never be like this again," Ford said. "I don't care how fancy those other (multiplexes) get. The charm of movie theaters like this will never be the same."

Ford added, "The folks who never came here missed something."

Johanna Epperson recalled when she was homeless and had nowhere to go except for the Forest.

"It was Easter and raining," she said. "But I could come to the Forest and not feel alone. It felt like family."

She looked like she was about to cry. Mallette did too.

32

Hamden Woman Made History as a "Freedom Rider"

(March 21, 2004)

IT SEEMS LIKE SUCH A LONG TIME AGO WHEN BLACK PEOPLE IN THE South were not allowed to drink from the same water fountain as whites, nor sit at a lunch counter.

But that's the way it was just a little over 40 years ago, and Lula White, now 65 and retired, vividly remembers "the indignity" of it all.

She also will never forget the sight and sound of a howling mob of racists trying to overturn the bus she was in as a "Freedom Rider."

Sitting on a couch in the house she now shares with her sister in a quiet Hamden neighborhood, White is far removed from the tumult and the shouting that made international news. She is soft-spoken and modest about what she did when she was 22 years old.

What led to her being on that bus, making history?

She was born in Alabama and moved to New Haven at age six. Her childhood in the South, plus visits there afterward, provided painful experiences with segregation.

"I knew about having to sit at the back of the bus and in the balcony of movie theaters and not being able to use the swimming pool or the library," she said.

White and her family also were not allowed to use bathrooms in gas stations.

Lula White outside her home in Hamden. (*New Haven Register* photographer Chris Volpe)

"I remember being outraged that we had to bring our own toilet paper and go out in the woods, the indignity of it," she said.

White noted the North was also segregated, but more subtly. "There were lots of jobs and houses blacks couldn't get."

After she graduated from Hillhouse High School, White went to the University of Chicago to study history. Eventually she returned to New Haven and taught at Lee High School.

But historic events intruded after college. In May 1961, "Freedom Riders" began moving through the South, challenging discrimination in interstate bus travel. In Alabama a group of them were savagely beaten.

"What motivated me," White said, "was seeing the photograph of the bus burning. I saw that picture and I just knew more people had to go. If they didn't go, the South would win."

When I asked whether she had been worried about her own physical safety, White replied, "I did consider that, because I am somewhat of a coward. But I just decided I had to go."

White and eight other "Freedom Riders," some white and some black, got on a bus in Nashville, Tenn., bound for Jackson, Miss.

The plan was for the whites to go into the bus station waiting room for blacks and for the blacks to go into the waiting room for whites.

But on the way to Jackson, while the bus was stopped, she said, "a group of whites tried to turn our bus over."

"There were about 50 to 60 of them, and they were shouting racial epithets," she said.

"It was scary," she added, "because we didn't know what would happen if the bus got turned over. They were rocking it for 10 or 15 minutes."

Finally the bus drove on and the group headed for another encounter in Jackson, where an even larger crowd awaited them.

"They were surrounding the bus station, howling and screaming," she said.

But White and the eight others walked off the bus, past the mob and into the bus station's waiting rooms. They were quickly arrested.

Although the charge was merely breach of peace, after being convicted they were sent to a maximum security prison for two months.

"They took away my Bible and Shakespeare books," she said.

On several occasions later in her life, White again was arrested for her beliefs. In 1975, she and 77 other New Haven school teachers were charged with participating in an illegal strike. Last fall, she was arrested with many others for blocking traffic during the strike by Yale workers.

But being a "Freedom Rider" clearly exposed her to the greatest danger. I asked her if she knew she had done something heroic. White replied, "When I was younger, I didn't think so.

"But the older I get, the more I think it was courageous," she said. "I'm getting prouder as I get older."

33

Let's Fire Up a Big, Fat Stogie. You Got a Problem With That?

(May 30, 2004)

THE PIGEONS AND CIGAR SMOKERS REJOICE EVERY MORNING (EXCEPT Sundays) when they see Fran Squillo Vessichio and her husband "Big John" Vessichio pull up to the curb outside the Squillo Distribution Co. on State Street for another fun day's work.

Feed the birds, sell a few cigars, shoot the breeze with the neighbors and customers. It's been this way for 44 years here, and for decades before that on Wallace Street.

"My great-uncle Salvatore Apuzzo opened his cigar and candy store on Wallace Street in the late 1920s or before," Fran said. "Then my dad (Angelo Squillo) took it over."

In those days, Squillo's Cigars were distributed all over Connecticut, driven to stores by the family.

This was long before doctors raised concerns about the health effects of smoking and second-hand smoke. Now, when a reporter walks in the door at Squillo's, that scribe will bring up the subject, as I eventually did.

"Wanna cigar?" was the first thing "Big John" said to me.

I told him I don't smoke. He gave me a sorrowful look but that didn't stop him nor Fran from carrying on in their customary way. Both of them smoked cigarettes off-and-on during the interview.

It was just after ten o'clock on a Wednesday morning but already the regulars were stopping in to browse amongst the array of cigar boxes. The Vessichios greeted them all like old friends, which they are.

"We treat our customers like family," Fran said. "I've walked into places where there's nobody to help you, nobody says hello. We treat this as our home because we spend so many hours here."

A few minutes later, an employee from J.P. Dempsey's across the street came in with a tall bag full of bread loaves.

"Those pigeons better not be fussy!" the woman said, then departed.

"The bread's a little burnt," Fran explained. "They don't want to serve it to their customers."

Instead the pigeons and starlings and sparrows would get it, tossed to them by the Vessichios during their lunch break when they sit outside their store.

But at mid-morning the pigeons were already helping themselves outside. "I buy birdseed for them," Fran said. "Fifty-pound bags."

Fran and "Big John" have names for the pigeons. "Hopalong" has a limp and "the General" is missing a leg.

John Cavaliere, who owns Lyric Hall Antiques & Restoration next door, popped in to visit and offer a testimonial.

"This is the anchor of State Street," he said, gesturing around the little place with its assorted cigar-store Indians.

"It's the last bastion of New Haven, the hold-out," Cavaliere added. "We guard it jealously because it's like an ecosystem."

Cavaliere said every morning he puts out a milk carton to save the Vessichios a parking spot because "'Big John' doesn't walk so well . . . They are a civilizing influence in the neighborhood and the city."

When people from out of town visit, Cavaliere said, they say things such as "We don't have anything like this in Westport." Even Greenwich Village, he said, has lost such funky institutions.

But how can Squillo's survive in a health-conscious world with fewer and fewer smokers?

"Business is steady," Fran said, noting they own the building, so rent isn't an issue. "But we're not getting rich. It's a tough business.

Fran Squillo Vessichio and her husband "Big John" Vessichio at their cigar store. (*New Haven Register* photographer Melanie Stengel)

"I think in years to come you won't see this (kind of store) anymore," she said.

Things got a little testy when I brought up the health issue.

"We live in America," Fran said. "The government shouldn't be telling people what to do with their lives, just because a handful of people say 'This isn't good for you, this is going to kill you.'"

According to Fran, whether an individual is harmed by smoking "depends on the person. It's all in the way a person is genetically made up."

I could see there was no point in debating science and statistics, so I asked about the future. Squillo's Cigars are still being made, by an outside company and Fran said, "We'll just keep on going until we can't anymore.

"What are we gonna do?" she asked. "Stay home? This is like home."

34

At the Edge of an Abyss, a Second Chance at Life is Found

(October 17, 2004)

PAUL HAMMER DOESN'T REMEMBER VERY MUCH ABOUT THAT AWFUL day last May when he went to the summit of East Rock and jumped off the cliff in a desperate attempt to end his life.

Several weeks later, as he was continuing his long recovery at Yale-New Haven Hospital, his loved ones and doctors finally told him what he had done.

"I'd thought I was in a bicycle accident," said Hammer, an avid biker. "I said, 'What? Me? Jump off a cliff? I'm afraid of heights!'"

Hammer's sense of humor has always helped him and it's one of the things I treasure about him. We have been friends for more than 25 years.

Because he had seemed so upbeat, I was shocked and saddened when I learned he was the man who had jumped off that cliff. Before that, I had heard only initial news reports.

When I visited him in the hospital a couple of days later, he was heavily medicated and speaking incoherently. He had fractured his skull, shattered a knee cap and broken his leg.

He had cuts and bruises all over his face, and his right eye was swollen shut. I doubted he would ever see out of that eye again.

And so it has been wonderful seeing him return to being the Paul Hammer I remember. His eyes are fine and there are no scars on his face.

But what matters most is his spirits are high, his brain is fine and he is smiling and laughing again.

"It's a miracle I'm alive," he told me. "God must have other plans for me."

He knows he was very lucky. "I survived jumping 400 feet. I don't know where I landed, but there was some brush to cushion my fall."

He added, "I have more to do. I'm 48 and I intend to do a lot of things in my 50s."

His girlfriend, who asked not to have her name used, told me, "He's a miracle man."

Paul Hammer outside his home in Branford in October 2004. (*New Haven Register* photographer Aaron Flaum)

The day after Hammer jumped, my office received a fax from Melanie Barocas Mayer of Guilford. She noted, "Paul has dedicated his life to helping this community" through his work at social service agencies and theaters.

"But he could no longer afford his medication," she said.

"Yesterday he spoke to my husband, Rick Mayer, and explained he needed medical benefits and may have to give up his community work to take a job at Stop & Shop just so he could afford his bipolar medication," she wrote.

"The last thing Rick said to Paul was, 'God bless you, Paul. Hang in there; things will get better.'"

She said Hammer's plight shows the critical need for affordable health care, and not just for the poor.

That was how I learned my friend has bipolar disorder, characterized by emotional highs (manias) and lows (depressions).

"It can be treated," he told me. "But getting the right combination of medication for each person is hard."

When he jumped, he said, "I was running out of medication. I had run out of unemployment benefits and a financial opportunity had fallen through. I fell into a deep depression."

Hammer does remember telling a Yale student at the top of East Rock he was going to jump off the edge and kill himself. The student couldn't talk him out of it.

"I remember looking over the cliff and saying, 'No, I can't do this,'" Hammer told me. "But I was so determined because I was so depressed."

He credits support from his family and friends for his recovery. He added, "I do believe a higher power was holding me in the light."

In addition to his girlfriend and his father, who stayed near him after his suicide attempt, Hammer noted: "I have a son, who I love dearly, and other people I love."

He wants to get work helping others with mental illness, "to give something back." He hopes to move from Harbor Health Apartments in Branford, which houses people coping with mental illness, and get an apartment in East Haven.

He said surviving and recovering from the jump "has made me look at the future with optimism."

Hammer is bicycling again and said it feels wonderful.

When I asked what he will tell people in trouble, he replied, "If you're considering taking your own life, don't do it. There's hope out there from other people who've been faced with the same feelings.

"But give yourself that gift of time," he added. "Time is the greatest healer. Because people will come to their senses. I wish I'd done that on that day.

"I feel very fortunate," he said, "to be able to look forward to the rest of my life."

I slipped off my yellow Lance Armstrong bracelet—which reads "Live strong"—and gave it to my old friend. I told him he deserves to wear it for the rest of his long and meaningful life.

35

Great Teachers, Like Great Art, Remain Forever Loved

(December 12, 2004)

WHEN I TOLD YALE'S ART HISTORIAN VINCENT SCULLY I WAS EAGER TO attend his final lecture of the semester (and perhaps his final one ever at Yale), he replied, "There may not be many people there."

Once again this modest but distinguished man had underestimated his appeal and importance.

As he walked down the aisle of the auditorium at Yale Law School last Monday morning, Scully was doubtless astonished to see at least 100 people there, including not just students but also other professors and local residents.

The word had spread around the campus and city that Scully, 84, might take a sabbatical next year.

And since he spends his spring semesters teaching at the University of Miami, who knew when any of us would ever have another opportunity to behold a Scully lecture?

The Sterling Professor Emeritus of the History of Art began teaching at Yale in 1947. Through the years his legendary lectures have attracted ever-larger audiences.

People everywhere are catching on to our local gem. Last month he went to the White House to receive the National Medal of the Arts.

Scully was born in New Haven, attended Hillhouse High School and entered Yale at 16. He has been a lifelong defender of this city's architectural heritage.

Scully's love for his old town is clear in a new book he has co-written, "Yale in New Haven: Architecture & Urbanism."

The other authors include Scully's wife Catherine Lynn, who teaches at the Yale School of Art and Architecture, and two of Scully's former students, Paul Goldberger and Erik Vogt.

Scully never hesitated to fight the good preservation fight when local treasures were threatened. Along with other local heroes such as Margaret Flint, Scully opposed the redevelopment schemes of the 1950s and '60s.

"What if all those connectors had gone through!" he wrote after citing boneheaded plans by the administration of Mayor Richard C. Lee to put highways through irreplaceable sanctuaries, including East Rock Park and Wooster Square.

But preservationists were not able to stop the destruction of what Scully recognized as a viable and integrated enclave: the Oak Street neighborhood.

He said all those planners intended the connectors "to cut the city to ribbons to permit the car to run free."

"The experience of the past 30 years has shown that everything the DOT (state Department of Transportation) and New Haven Redevelopment wanted to do was utterly wrong in every way," Scully wrote.

In more recent years, Scully has fought against the proposed Galleria Mall at Long Wharf (IKEA went there instead) and the planned demolition of four historic buildings at Yale Divinity School. Scully won that fight, too, after threatening to leave the university if that plan went through.

But those of us lucky enough to be in that auditorium last Monday were on hand to hear Scully rhapsodize on Michelangelo for his "Introduction to the History of Art" course.

Alan Plattus, one of Scully's former students who was inspired to become an architect, told me: "Vince has always argued that architecture and cities are a great dialogue between generations. He, too, has become a huge part of that dialogue."

Plattus added, "As architects, we seem to be perpetually thirsty, and Vince continues to be one of the great 'wells' in an increasingly dry landscape."

In the following 50 minutes, Scully, working with slides of Michelangelo's David, the Pieta and the Vault of the Sistine Chapel, expertly and passionately explained the genius in such beauty.

"To think that this is marble!" Scully marveled as he showed the Pieta sculpture. "You think of a baby's hands—so soft."

He wound up by noting how such artists show us "the splendor of the human body." And then he was finished.

"Thank you," he murmured as the applause began. "You have been a great class." Then he almost ran up the aisle as the audience rose for a standing ovation.

Five minutes later, I found him in a hallway. "I'm sorry," he said. "I have to get out when they do that."

Scully said he will "try to take a year off" but he doesn't know what will come after that.

"When do you stop?" he asked. "I don't know how I can ever give up teaching. But I have to stop sometime."

No matter what he decides, we have been lucky to have him with us, like one of this city's fine old works of architecture.

36

Thompson's Outspoken Activism
Made Political Journalism Matter

(February 25, 2005)

THIS HAS BEEN A SAD, WISTFUL WEEK, MY MIND FILLED WITH MULTIPLE memorable images of a lost outlaw.

I see him sitting on a stage, grinning, laughing, swigging from his bottle of Wild Turkey, firing off one-liners at his enemies.

This strangest, strongest memory comes from a wonderfully bizarre night at the University of Hartford in June 1981 when the guest lecturer was "Dr. Hunter S. Thompson."

Even then, at 42, he was coasting on his reputation as the "gonzo journalist," a participatory writer who had revolutionized presidential campaign coverage with his savage, dead-on attacks on certain candidates.

In his 1972 book "Fear and Loathing on the Campaign Trail," Thompson wrote that Sen. Hubert Humphrey "has always campaigned like a rat in heat."

Thompson also observed that President Richard M. Nixon represented "that dark, venal and incurably violent side of the American character."

When I saw those words blown up in a pull quote from Rolling Stone magazine, I taped them to the wall of my college dormitory. This was the guy who made me want to go into journalism.

He made it fun. He made it matter.

A decade later, when Nixon was gone but Ronald Reagan had replaced him in the White House, I had a reporter's job at the *New Haven Register*

Hunter S. Thompson at the University of Hartford. (*New Haven Register* reporter Lynne Garnett)

and I had a fun assignment: cover the Thompson speech at the University of Hartford.

When he came on stage, dressed in a racing car jacket, he had not just the Wild Turkey but also a glass of wine and a tin box containing freshly rolled joints of marijuana.

He was there, he announced, to have fun.

But the students' questions made it hard for him to have any fun at all, because they kept asking him about the state of the nation.

"A gang of savage monsters is running the country," he said. "Reagan matters about as much as Dean Martin. If you believe he's in charge of anything, you're really missing the point."

He also offered a history lesson. "In the '60s, because of the intense activism, there was always the sense that we were right. They might cut us off at the pass and beat us, but we would prevail."

Then he added, "Suddenly there is a chill in the air. I don't see any sense now in my going out on the barricades."

Yes, even then he had become a kind of caricature, a cartoon figure. Speaking of the "Duke" character in Garry Trudeau's "Doonesbury," Thompson told the crowd: "Given one slight change in the legal interpretation, I'd have that little half-wit b----- working in my yard for the rest of his life."

Before he left the stage, he said, "I've always felt like an outlaw, and I feel comfortable to go to my grave that way."

And then some supreme serendipity came my way. I ducked into the bathroom and beheld, emerging from a stall, the gonzo man himself.

Others gathered around him and we had a spontaneous b.s. session. Thompson pulled out one of his joints and passed it around our circle.

Still the students kept trying to resuscitate their savior. "You've got to start writing about the political scene again," one of them said. "Reagan's in the White House. We need you."

Thompson shrugged and said, "I'm not 20 years old anymore. I've been to the well—and the water is poison."

Fast forward to April 1989, the Palace Theater, New Haven. Thompson is on stage again, drinking Chivas Regal, more rambling in his responses to the crowd but still defiant and idealistic.

Abbie Hoffman, the '60s activist with a sense of fun, had died a week earlier. A suicide.

"Abbie was always on the right side. He was funny and he died with his boots on, in bed," Thompson said. "You try that."

When an 18-year-old asked Thompson if it was worth trying to make a difference in the '90s, Thompson quieted the hooting cynics in the audience.

"If you people realized how much fun it is to make a difference," he said. "We ran several presidents out of the White House. Has it ever occurred to you that you could do that?

"It should occur to you," he said. "If you're really angry about something, a lot of people will go with you. We've lost that sense of possibility."

Because he felt this even more strongly 16 years later, because it wasn't fun anymore, Thompson committed his last outlaw act and put a gun to his head.

But let's remember what he told us as well as what he wrote.

37

This is the End of the Quest to Find Woman Who Lit Morrison's Fire

(March 20, 2005)

AFTER TWO YEARS OF SEARCHING, THE DOORS' MYSTERY WOMAN, WHO was backstage at the old New Haven Arena, has been found.

But still she refuses to talk about what happened when she had that famous encounter with the Doors' legendary lead singer Jim Morrison.

The former Sandy Spodnik lives in the Danbury area and at this point does not wish to discuss her role in cultural history.

"I don't have anything to say to you or anyone on the subject you mentioned," she wrote me in response to a letter I sent her. "Please don't contact me again."

Because of the request in her letter, I will not reveal her married name or address.

I wasn't the one who tracked her down. The credit goes to Charles Morano, a retired police detective who used to work for the Monroe Police Department. He is now employed by a private detective/security agency.

My mission to speak with the Doors' mystery woman began in July 2003 when I was reading archival clippings about the band's aborted show at the Arena on December 9, 1967.

The Doors never got to finish their performance because New Haven police turned on the lights, came on stage and dragged Morrison off to jail.

Jim Morrison's mug shot. (*New Haven Register* file photo)

He was charged with breach of peace, resisting arrest and "performing an indecent and immoral exhibition."

Those events were set into motion before the show by Morrison's attempt to make out in a dressing room shower with Spodnik.

Tommy Janette, who now works for the Narcotics Officers Association in Wallingford, was also backstage that night with his band, Tommy and the Rivieras. They were the opening act.

Janette told me his band's new uniforms, featuring black leather pants and "white Tom Jones silk shirts" had been delivered that night but they had no pockets. Thus the band members had put their wallets and cash on the table in the dressing room.

"When I looked into the shower/bathroom," Janette said, "I saw a long-haired hippie with his back to me, making out with a girl. I didn't know it was Morrison."

Janette recalled the young woman was "a pretty brunette."

Concerned about the band's money, Janette told his guitar player Buddy Tinari to get the two young lovers out of there. When Morrison snarled an obscenity at Tinari, Janette asked a police officer on duty to clear the shower.

A fight ensued, Morrison got sprayed with Mace and the "pretty brunette" ran off, lost to history.

But before she left the Arena, police got her name. She was identified in the police report as "Sandy Spodniak," 18, a Southern Connecticut State College student. This was long before it became a university.

The police let Morrison take the stage that night because they didn't want the crowd to riot. But when he started recounting the backstage fight during his performance, mocking "this little man in a little blue suit," the police stopped the show.

After I wrote my first "where is she now and who is she?" column, former Arena employee Gary Deleone showed me a copy of that police report, enabling me to learn the identity of "Sandy Spodniak." (It was hard to read the copy; the name looked like "Spodniak" or "Spodnick.")

I made dozens of calls, following many false leads, in my attempt to find this woman. But when a Doors book researcher and Morano read my second column that summer, Morano was hired by the researcher and went to work.

Morano said the breakthrough came after he went through many phone book directories from the 1960s through 2003. He then made about 60 calls to all the Spodniak and Spodnik spelling combinations. It turned out her maiden name was Sandy Spodnik.

Morano said his friend on the New Haven Police Department helped him find Spodnik's brother, "who gave her up."

Morano, a longtime fan of the Doors and a member of their fan club in the 1960s, said the search was "a fun adventure."

But he said the former Sandy Spodnik also refused to speak with the Doors' biographer.

"Sandy told them that when she is ready, she will talk," Morano said.

Only she knows when, if ever, that day will come.

38

A Funny Thing Happened on the Way Home From Comiskey Park

(April 10, 2005)

ON A RECENT RAINY SATURDAY MORNING IN A COMFORTABLE, UNPRE-
tentious home overlooking the woods and streams of Stamford, Phil Linz
was playing "Take Me Out to the Ball Game" on his harmonica.

As an encore, Linz played "Mary Had a Little Lamb." For me, it was
a beautiful and historic moment.

Why historic? It helps if you were a New York Yankees fan in 1964.

On August 20 of that year, Linz, then a utility infielder for the Yankees, and his manager, Yogi Berra, had a legendary encounter that gal-
vanized the slumping team and eventually helped Linz launch a second
career.

It happened on the team bus after the Yanks had left Comiskey Park.
They had lost a doubleheader to the Chicago White Sox and were on a
four-or-five-game losing streak.

Berra was brooding in his seat at the front of the bus. But Linz had
just bought his first harmonica and he wanted to try it out.

The tune he chose was, you guessed it, "Mary Had a Little Lamb."

Berra stood up and growled, "Knock it off."

Linz turned to Mickey Mantle and asked, "What'd he say?"

Mantle answered: "He said, 'Play it louder.'"

And so Linz kept playing, at a higher volume. Berra stalked up the
aisle.

Phil Linz at his home in Stamford. (*New Haven Register* photographer Keelin Daly)

Linz well remembers what happened next. "Yogi said, 'Shove that harmonica up . . .' You know where. I flipped it at him and said, 'You do it.' He threw it back at me. It whizzed past my ear."

Linz said that the next day he apologized to Berra and they hugged.

"Yogi said to me, 'I've got to fine you something because the writers are doing all these stories about it. Is $200 OK?'"

Linz, whose salary that year was $14,000, said $200 was not a problem. He said when Ralph Houk became manager the following year, he gave him a raise to $20,200. Houk said the $200 was for "music lessons."

That $200 was a bargain. After the story broke, the Hohner Harmonica Co. people offered Linz $10,000 for ads showing him playing their instrument. The ad copy said: "Play it, Phil."

All was soon forgiven anyway because after that squabble the team loosened up and started to win. They zoomed up from third place and clinched the pennant. "Suddenly it was OK to play the harmonica," Linz said.

Now, at age 66, he plays it when stuck in traffic on his daily commute to New York, where he is a vice president for the Stewart Title Insurance Co.

"It's a great instrument; great for relaxing," he said. Playing one of his originals, all of which he calls "Phil's Tune," he noted that his two cats "love it." He added, "Watch their ears."

His wife Lynn, however, had left the room.

Linz is so intent in encouraging others to play harmonica that he gave me one, with an instruction sheet.

"Everything I've ever gotten is from the harmonica," he said. "I saved enough (from the endorsement) to open a restaurant in New York called Mr. Laffs."

But that was also the end of his time with the Yankees. In the summer of 1965, when team officials learned Linz was planning to open a bar-restaurant, they asked him not to do it because it wouldn't fit the Yankee image.

Linz went ahead anyway. The day before he opened his place he was traded to the Phillies.

After the 1967 season, Linz was traded to the Mets. One of their coaches was: Berra.

"Yogi could've held that harmonica thing against me," Linz said. "But he was instrumental in getting me to the Mets."

After an unremarkable year with those Mets, Linz retired from baseball. He was 28.

He spent the next 23 years as a bar-restaurant owner.

"I had to improvise," he said, a theme of his entire life. "I tried the rock music format, then disco. It's like I do with my harmonica; I kept hitting different notes."

But when his nightclubs fizzled out, he faced another tough transition. "I had no skills."

Linz took an entry-level job with Liberty Mutual and discovered, "It's nice to deal with sober people." His third career had begun.

Linz remains "a die-hard Yankee fan" but is dismayed about baseball's steroids scandal.

He recalls playing with Roger Maris, who in 1961 set the home run record by hitting 61.

"Roger should be reinstated as the home run king," Linz said. "How many homers would (Mark) McGwire or (Barry) Bonds have hit without steroids? Probably 40 or 50."

Later Linz showed me his basement of memorabilia. My fantasy morning was interrupted only once, when he said I look like former Red Sox pitcher Bill "Spaceman" Lee. Then he asked me, in a shattering moment, if I'm a Red Sox fan.

39

City Tailor Well Suited to Tell Holocaust Story

(May 6, 2005)

THE HORRIBLE, UNBELIEVABLE IMAGES ARE STILL IN SIDNEY GLUCKS-man's head, but he has beautiful memories, too, of an adopted "brother" and of liberation.

Sixty years ago this week, on May 5, 1945, Glucksman finally walked out of the gates of Dachau, the notorious Nazi death camp. He was free.

It was a walk he had never believed could happen.

"I remember every day," said Glucksman, 77, as he sat in Sidney's Tailoring & Cleaning on Chapel Street in New Haven. "I live with it every single day."

Many survivors of those experiences gathered Thursday in Europe for Holocaust Remembrance Day. But Glucksman was not among them.

"I am not ready," he said.

One of the people who did make it over there was Jerome Klein, the U.S. Army soldier who took Glucksman under his wing on "Liberation Day" and has been his friend ever since.

When they first encountered one another at Dachau, Klein beheld an emaciated 17-year-old kid who had typhoid. Klein disinfected him with a powder.

"I didn't speak English but he started speaking to me in German, which I did know," Glucksman recalled.

Sidney Glucksman at his tailor shop. (*New Haven Register* photographer Peter Casolino)

"I thought, 'Jewish soldiers in an American army?'" Glucksman added, "I couldn't believe it."

Klein took Glucksman out of the camp, offered him a shower (his first in years) and gave him one of his Army uniforms.

"That was the day I took off my striped 'uniform,'" Glucksman said. "And I became like newborn. I was able to look like a human being."

His descent into six years surrounded by the madness and inhumanity of labor and death camps began in 1939 when the Germans invaded Poland. (A warning to readers: If you are not able to deal with vivid descriptions of cruelty, you should stop reading this now).

"The Germans took out all these old people from the synagogue and lined them up against the wall," Glucksman recalled. "They machine-gunned them down, one by one. They were still wearing their praying shawls.

"Whoever was Jewish (and able to work) they put on the trucks," Glucksman said. "They took us to a labor camp.

"I thought they were going to bring us back that night," he added. "But I never saw since then my parents or my brother or sister."

He said the Germans didn't load his brother or sister onto the trucks because they weren't old enough to work. Glucksman was 12.

"What saved my life," Glucksman said, "was because I knew how to sew."

A year after he was sent to that labor camp, Glucksman recognized some new arrivals from his hometown.

"I asked them if my parents were all right," he said. "They told me, 'No, nobody's alive.'"

In 1943, Glucksman was sent to the Gross-Rosen camp, where he witnessed atrocities day by day.

"They brought in women in boxcars with their children in their arms," he said. "They lined them up and told them to place their babies on the ground.

"The women had to take off all their clothes. Then they were led off. They thought they were going to take a shower. But they never came out."

As for the babies, Glucksman said, "The Germans put them in bags and hit them against the concrete walls. We had to dispose of the bodies."

His job also was to load the bodies of the gas chamber victims onto wagons and take them to the crematorium. "Bodies were piled up by the thousands."

He added, "I could smell the burning bodies. I thought, 'I'll be dead tomorrow. I'm going up that chimney.'"

But as long as he could work, the Germans kept him alive, eventually sending him to Dachau.

And then at last came that day when the Germans vanished and the camp workers saw U.S. Army tanks smash down Dachau's gates. "We were dancing," he said.

Klein kept track of Glucksman during his years at a displaced-persons camp. That's where Glucksman met his future wife, Libby, who had spent the war sheltered in forests.

Klein paid Glucksman's way to America, where he was reunited with Libby and married her. They moved to New Haven in 1949, opened the tailor shop and raised two daughters.

Standing alongside her husband this week, she noted he continues to speak about his war experiences in schools, libraries and homes for the aged.

"He says, 'After I'm gone, nobody's going to know.' In some places they don't believe it."

Glucksman said, "People ask me, 'How come you're alive? How were you able to make it through?' I tell them, 'God must have wanted it this way, so I could be a witness to it.'"

The door opened and in walked Steve Lillquist, whose father Arthur was in the infantry squad that liberated Glucksman. Both Lillquists are customers.

"That's why I light up," Glucksman said, patting Lillquist. "I see people like this guy and it makes me feel younger, stronger. This is my therapy."

40

Welcome to Circus Minimus, Nearly 80 Years in the Making

(June 12, 2005)

ON A FATEFUL SUMMER'S DAY IN 1926, A NINE-YEAR-OLD BOY NAMED William Brinley went with his dad to see the Christy Bros. Circus, which had come to their town, Wallingford.

The boy was so mesmerized and enchanted by what he saw that he announced: "When I grow up, I'll have a circus of my own."

Young Brinley was thinking he would own a real circus. But what he did instead was create two renditions of his own miniature circus, piece by piece, to astound and delight the public.

This lifelong work, an unforgettable twin exhibit of folk art, is still in progress, 79 years later, and on full display at the Barnum Museum in Bridgeport.

The museum's red-and-yellow flyer touts the first-floor miniature circus as "amazing." It surely is, and so is its creator.

He is 87 now, and every Wednesday he makes the drive to Bridgeport from his home in Meriden in order to work some more on his circus.

"I'd come here more often," he told me when I met him there last Wednesday. "But I have to take care of my wife, Madeleine." She is in poor health.

And then he climbed over the railing to get to his creation: a sprawling network of tents, railroad cars, animals, spectators and acts.

William Brinley at the Barnum Museum. (*New Haven Register* photographer Peter Hvizdak)

Some of the tiny performers are motorized and thus in constant whirling motion. Your eyes are drawn to the ladies riding bareback on ponies; the acrobats on the high wire; the strong man lifting a barbell; and the sword swallower whose sword moves up and down into his mouth.

Thousands of carved spectators observe all of this. When I asked Brinley how many audience members he has made, he said, "Oh, about 8,000. I try to make each of them a little different."

He said it's the same for the animals. "Each one is individual, which is how it should be."

Brinley picked up one of his ringmasters. "That's Marlene," he said affectionately, meaning the actress Marlene Dietrich.

He said that in 1949 when he was exhibiting his show for Cole Bros. Circus in Las Vegas, Dietrich was a guest ringmaster.

"So I made this one of her," Brinley recalled. "When I showed it to her, she said, 'Oh, baby! Wonderful!'"

His circus-carving talent also launched him on a road tour with cowboy actors William Boyd (Hopalong Cassidy) and Clayton Moore ("The

Lone Ranger"). In 1950, Brinley exhibited his work on "The Ed Sullivan Show."

All of this came from many years of meticulous research and craftwork.

"When I was a kid, about 12, the circus came to New Haven, in a tent on Dixwell Avenue," he said.

"My father would drop me off there on his way to work. I had a little Brownie camera, a measuring stick and a pad. I'd stay all day, taking measurements and pictures."

What did he use for raw materials? "I cut cheese boxes in half to make band wagons. My first railroad cars were made from orange crates."

Brinley added, "The merchants in Wallingford saved them for me. They called me 'that crazy kid with the circus.'"

Other kids laughed at him for his consuming hobby. A sign posted at the museum quotes Brinley: "When I got hired to exhibit my circus in Atlantic City, they paid me a lot of money ($50 a week). Who's laughing now? You have to stick to what you love to do."

When he served in the U.S. Army Air Corps during World War II, he kept on carving, sending the pieces home. "All I needed was a jigsaw and a knife."

But what's even more amazing is this: Brinley has another circus upstairs, on the museum's third floor.

He took me up there, where I beheld this second giant all-encompassing landscape of tents, railroad cars, performers, animals and more.

This is his original work, begun when he was nine. He pointed out the first band wagon he made out of a cheese box and the first railroad car, created from one of those orange crates.

Brinley kept doing this circus until 1968 (42 years of devotion), when he donated it to the museum. Then he started work on the second one—36 years so far and he's not done yet.

At home in Meriden he is still carving.

"When I finish a piece," he said, "I feel I've made something from days gone by."

Although he admits his hands now shake somewhat from advancing age, he can't imagine ever stopping this work. "I've got so many more things to do."

Circus owner P.T. Barnum himself would applaud such determined showmanship. A sign on the museum's first floor quotes Brinley: "I hope my God-given talents will give enjoyment to children of all ages as they come to see the circus."

41

Like the Perennials He Sells, He Just Keeps Coming Back

(October 2, 2005)

FOR MORE THAN 65 YEARS ANGELO DESORBO HAS BEEN THE KING OF the corner at Kimberly Avenue and Ella Grasso Boulevard in New Haven.

The king, who is 97, still holds court, although he has moved his business a few yards down Kimberly Avenue onto the sidewalk, and his flowering plant customers now come to his "throne" because his legs have given out.

But DeSorbo's feisty spirit is still going strong.

"This is my life," he said, gesturing toward the racks of plants. "I'm not doing it for the money."

DeSorbo is supported by his trusty sidekick Henry Scirocco, who is only 77 and thus can still walk around, maneuvering the flower carts. Scirocco is the heir to the throne.

DeSorbo also has a crew of neighborhood friends and helpers, along with his corps of aging but devoted customers.

Edward Giovannini, who owns Gumbo's Auto Sales across the street, stopped in to visit Wednesday morning and to reminisce.

"I've seen Angelo here for more than 55 years, ever since I was a kid," Giovannini said.

He remembers when DeSorbo's place on the corner was called the Kimberly Open Air Market and you could buy groceries and liquor there.

Asked for the secret of DeSorbo's longevity, Giovannini replied, "Fruit! Every time you went in there he'd have an apple or pear in his mouth."

Frank Johnson was also on hand, shooting the breeze and helping out with any small tasks.

"He has a heart," Johnson said of DeSorbo. "If you need anything, he'll give it to you."

"He got me off the bottle in '96," Johnson said. "He gave me guidance. He gave me wisdom. I promised his wife I'd keep an eye on him."

"I lost my Gladys four years ago," DeSorbo told me. "A beautiful woman. Beautiful. She was French. We were married 65 years."

They had two kids but both have moved far away. DeSorbo's niece, Catherine DeSorbo, drives him to work every morning and a friend drives him home.

Home is now an apartment in West Haven, where he lives alone. "I used to live there," he said, pointing to the house behind his plants stand.

I sold everything 15 to 20 years ago," he said. "I pay rent now. I'm here seven days a week, usually nine in the morning 'til about one o'clock.

"If you knew how many kisses I get from women!" he told me. "That's the name of the game."

Scirocco said of DeSorbo, "He used to be a famous tap dancer. People threw pennies and nickels his way."

Looking down at his legs, DeSorbo said, "They don't talk to me no more. I wore them out."

But he added, "God gave me strength. I always had good health.

"I have a good appetite," he explained. "I have my beer, I have my Scotch—not much."

DeSorbo said he has no hobbies but he noted, "I'm a Yankees man. I used to have a box seat in Yankee Stadium."

When I asked him what famous players he had met, he said, "The catcher, Yogi, what was his last name?"

"Berra," said Scirocco, who finishes many of DeSorbo's sentences for him.

On the side wall of the shack Scirocco built for DeSorbo to protect him from the cold, there is a Yankees clock and a photo of Babe Ruth. This presents a problem for Johnson.

"He's a Red Sox fan," Scirocco said, nodding darkly toward Johnson. "When the Sox lose, he doesn't come down here."

Johnson told me he can't bear to sit on "the Yankees side" of the shack.

Scirocco told me he has known DeSorbo for decades. But he didn't start coming to the corner regularly until his wife Patricia died eight years ago.

"I've been here ever since," he said. "Mostly I do it as a favor. I feel bad for him because he can't walk too good."

"This is his place when I go," DeSorbo said. But Scirocco said DeSorbo might outlast him.

Scirocco pulled me aside and said they have spats about where to set up the plants. "You can't change a dog's old ways," he noted.

When I asked how the business is doing, Scirocco replied, "Right now, lousy. People are all planted-out. We stay here 'til Christmas, then close for the winter."

Spring is the busy season for them. But Scirocco also noted, "A lot of the old-timers have passed away. They came faithfully, like clockwork. The young kids, they don't want to be bothered doing the planting."

Exactly how long has DeSorbo been holding down that corner? He doesn't know, but "Angelo 1940" is carved on the sidewalk and he said he was there even before then.

Asked if he wants to make it there to age 100, DeSorbo said, "I don't know. It's up to God."

42

Granddaughters Share Stories, Carry on the Babe's Legacy

(May 12, 2006)

WHEN I SAT DOWN WITH TWO OF BABE RUTH'S GRANDDAUGHTERS IN Wallingford earlier this week, they told me so many great baseball stories and colorful anecdotes that I decided I had to follow up my Wednesday news story with a bonus package here.

I liked both of them right away, even though Linda Ruth Tosetti of Durham is a Red Sox fan and I am a lifelong supporter of the New York Yankees.

I had learned about Tosetti's Sox loyalty two years ago when she appeared as a guest of honor at an oddly titled "Red Sox Nation" rally on the New Haven Green, organized by Red Sox management.

"New Haven is definitely Yankee territory," she admitted to me this week.

Tosetti also confessed that during the 1970s she was a huge fan of Yankees catcher Thurman Munson because he was a rebel. And she justly noted, "You've gotta respect the pinstripes and 'the house that Ruth built' (Yankee Stadium). Part of our hearts are there too."

Her sister, Ellen Ruth Hourigan of Wallingford, whose license plate is "Yanke3," said she roots for both the Yankees and the Red Sox. This seems like a crazy and impossible notion, especially in situations like this week when the rivals played each other. But she noted, "My grandfather played for both teams. I don't want to be a traitor to either of them."

Linda Ruth Tosetti (left) and Ellen Ruth Hourigan. (*New Haven Register* photographer Chris Volpe)

Hourigan told me she has not been to Yankee Stadium since 1988, when she attended a Babe Ruth commemoration at Old-Timers Day. She added wistfully, "I've never seen Monument Park," the collection of plaques behind center field that of course includes a prominent tribute to her grandpa.

"I'd like to see it once," she said. Her sister said she's working on this; she has been re-establishing contact with the Yankees organization.

Tosetti has made it to Monument Park. How she got there is one of her best stories.

On the day about 10 years ago when she tried to visit that shrine, she was accompanied by Paul Hopkins of Deep River. Students of history will recognize that name as the Washington Senators pitcher who in 1927 threw a ball to Ruth that he launched into the seats for his 59th homer of the season. At the time this was a new record.

When Tosetti mentioned Hopkins, I remembered interviewing him in Deep River in October 2003. At the time he was 99, which made him the world's oldest Major League Baseball player. Unfortunately, he died the next year before he could make it to 100.

Anyway, this remarkable pair of people naturally wanted to see Ruth's monument. But the gate was locked. The groundskeeper standing guard there was initially unsympathetic. In a scene reminiscent of the one from "The Wizard of Oz," he told them to go away, they couldn't get in, it wasn't open at that hour.

"But I'm Babe Ruth's granddaughter!" Tosetti told him.

"Can you prove it?" the groundskeeper asked.

"So I just pointed to my face," said Tosetti, who has that big open Ruthian smile. "And the guy said, 'Yeah, I guess you are!' and he opened the gate."

Once they got access, Tosetti and Hopkins couldn't resist walking onto the field and they even visited the pitcher's mound. "There I was with the pitcher who threw Babe's 59th home run, and it happened at Yankee Stadium," Tosetti said. "That's pretty cool!"

Even though Tosetti, 51, was born too late to meet her grandfather, she feels as if she knows him because of all the stories she has heard from ballplayers and fans of that era.

Quoting a former Negro Leagues star, Tosetti said, "Ted 'Double-Duty' Radcliffe told me, 'Your granddaddy, he was a good man. He was all for integrating baseball. He thought everybody should play baseball, that it was the cure for all ills.'"

Tosetti and Hourigan said Ruth not only delighted kids by visiting them at hospitals but he also insisted on touring a lepers' colony in Hawaii when other people were afraid to go there.

"You always hear about his carousing," Tosetti said. "But he was so much more than that."

As for the late-night binges, she said, "People don't know he had attention deficit hyperactivity disorder. He could only sleep for a couple of hours."

"Movies make him seem oafish," she said. "But he had manners. And he was a smart man. People sometimes used him but he knew it and helped them anyway. I wouldn't think that's the mark of a dumb man."

The sisters always delight in meeting kids who have read about Ruth in books and are awed to meet his granddaughters. Describing how the kids light up, Tosetti said, "We call it 'Babe Ruth eyes.'"

43

Welcome to the Greatest Basement of All Time

(January 28, 2007)

ANYONE WHO HAS THE RARE PRIVILEGE OF BEING INVITED DOWN INTO Rick Kaletsky's rec room/playroom/Muhammad Ali Museum will quickly realize: this man is a true fan.

Kaletsky prefers being called an "Aliologist." He has stated, "I am one of the greatest Aliologists going."

Kaletsky has been building an extensive collection of Ali memorabilia in his Bethany basement for decades. The museum and his self-published book, "Ali and Me: Through the Ropes" are, he asserts, "a labor of love."

He traces his admiration of the renowned boxer to 1962 when Kaletsky was a kid living in New Haven and the future Ali was still Cassius Clay. After Clay brashly predicted, "Archie Moore will fall in four," then made good on his prediction, Kaletsky was hooked.

"From the Moore fight on," he wrote in his book, "I've chased or followed 'The Champ' like a bee goes to honey."

His quest began a year later when Kaletsky decided to get "The Champ" on the phone.

"I was about 14," Kaletsky told me, "and I wanted to talk to him. I called directory assistance in Louisville (Kentucky) and he was listed! So I called him collect.

"He answered the call! And he was so nice. He was humble; I know that's an odd word for him. He said, 'You've heard about me all the way up there in Connecticut?'"

Rick Kaletsky in his Muhammad Ali Museum. (*New Haven Register* photographer Jeff Holt)

We had made it to "the lobby" of his museum, a small entryway, its walls covered with framed photos of Ali. Kaletsky picked up a toy microphone and announced: "Welcome to the Ali Museum!"

Then the curator escorted me inside. Ali's face and body were everywhere: on more framed pictures, on little figurines (one of which Kaletsky wound up for it to call out; "Who's the greatest?"), on DVDs, on record albums, on pennants, posters and postcards, on comic books, big books, magazines, shirts, shoe polish, cologne and Wheaties boxes.

Kaletsky is particularly proud of a shirt given to him by Ali's assistant trainer, Drew Brown. It has his nickname "Bundini" on the front and on the back is Ali's legendary phrase: "Float like a butterfly, sting like a bee." Kaletsky wore that shirt under his tuxedo the day he married his understanding wife, Laurie.

Another treasured item: a framed postcard addressed to Kaletsky, sent from Africa in 1974. This was shortly before Ali defeated George Foreman to win back the world championship. It reads: "Rick, this place isn't too bad, because Ali will win the championship." It was signed by Ali and his assistants.

Although Kaletsky didn't make it to that fight, he did see eight Ali bouts, including two encounters with George Frazier and his second fight with Leon Spinks.

"The first time I met him, he was training for the second Sonny Liston fight," Kaletsky said. "My uncle, Sam Cohen, a sportswriter, took me to see him in Chicopee, Mass."

Kaletsky shared a more intimate time with Ali in 1974 in Deer Lake, Pa. He was training for that Zaire bout with Foreman.

"I was alone with him," Kaletsky said. "He said softly, 'He's gonna be down for (the count of) 10.'" (Ali did knock him out, in the 8th round.)

When Ali recently turned 65, Kaletsky didn't call to wish him a happy birthday. "I didn't want to bug him."

But he added, "What I want on my tombstone is: 'I had the private number of Muhammad Ali and Sally's Apizza simultaneously.'"

I asked Kaletsky if his museum is open to the public. He said he will consider phone inquiries (203-393-1233) and offer a tour to somebody who buys his book ($15).

This led to another Ali anecdote. "When I published my book in 1982, I called him and told him I'd written it as a labor of love, dedicated to my dad (Louis). I said, 'I'll send you a copy. Please drop me a note afterward?' He said he would."

A few days later, at 1:30 a.m., Ali did call to say, "I got your book right here."

There is one more Ali story. It happened after that Spinks fight in New Orleans, September 15, 1978. Once again Ali had regained his heavyweight title. Using his chutzpah and connections, Kaletsky got into Ali's dressing room. Ali was screaming, "The greatest of all time!"

Later, with Ali only a few feet away, Kaletsky congratulated him. Recalling that moment, Kaletsky told me, "I was just looking around, absorbing it all, so I'd always have it."

And as Kaletsky wrote in his book, Ali "just kept saying over and over and over, in a voice that tried to bellow but could only strain: 'Of all time, of all time, of all time.'"

44

Positive Thinking and Good Shoes Get "Red" to the Post Office on Time

(September 23, 2007)

You've heard the old chestnut that "neither rain, nor snow, nor sleet, nor gloom of night shall keep the postman from his appointed rounds." It also holds true for a local mail handler.

One day at a time, one step after another, Donald "Red" Beatty keeps his "appointed rounds" by walking from his home in West Haven to the U.S. Postal Service building on Brewery Street in New Haven.

"I'm pretty steady," Beatty told me.

Yep, you could say that. The man is 66, and he has been making that walk for 40 years.

When one of his co-workers told me about Beatty ("He's like the iron man!"), I went to Brewery Street to meet this remarkable public servant.

Beatty got off work promptly at 1 p.m. (he had started, as he always does, at 4:30 a.m.) and he came out to see me with a smile, a warm greeting and a firm handshake.

I offered him a ride to West Haven and he suggested we go to his favorite diner there, the Duchess, so he could enjoy the meat loaf special.

"Usually I take the bus home," he said. "I figure I owe it to myself after working all day. In the old days I walked both ways. It keeps you young."

His once red hair (hence that nickname) has gone white. Besides that, he sure doesn't look 66.

While we rode over to the Duchess we discussed his childhood on Nicoll Street in New Haven, his move to Main Street in West Haven in 1971 with his parents and how the baseball player "Shoeless" Joe Jackson got his nickname by not wearing his cleats one day.

Beatty loves baseball, movies and old songs. He can readily recall details of long ago ballplayers or film stars.

He likes to read, too, but he told me he is dyslexic.

After we got to the Duchess and he greeted the waitresses by name and we ordered our meat loaf, I asked him if he had ever owned a car or driven one.

"A little bit, not too much," he said. "I've got a heavy foot" on the gas pedal.

He prefers the bus, the train and especially his own two feet.

"I get up maybe 1 or 1:30 (a.m.). It takes me about an hour and 10 minutes to get to work. If the weather's really bad, I might call a cab."

Then he told me about something I had heard from a co-worker. A few weeks ago, while Beatty was on his way to work, he was attacked.

"I was walking on Long Wharf Drive and I saw a fellow in a van. Something didn't look right.

"He came up behind me and he knocked me down. I was able to get back up; I was warding off the blows. He had a sharp stick and I knocked that away. The problem was I couldn't get my wallet out of my pocket right away."

But then the mugger got Beatty's wallet and left. Beatty, who scraped his knees in the struggle, continued walking to work and put in his full day as usual.

"I was able to forgive this fellow," Beatty told me. "I pray he turns to God and goes in the right direction."

Beatty said it was the first time anything like that had happened in 40 years. He has changed his route but vows, "I'll still do my walking."

"I've been fortunate," he added. "I couldn't ask for better people to work with."

His co-workers are amazed not just by his walking but by his reliability. They can't remember him taking a sick day, and neither can he, with just one exception in those 40 years.

"There was a snowstorm in '69 or '70. The snow was up to my thighs on East Street. I had to go back home, I confess."

But he made it to work during Hurricane Gloria in 1985. "I just had to watch out for the live wires."

On his days off, he goes for a walk to see a move at Showcase Cinemas in Orange. He used to go to West Haven's Forest Theater, but it's closed. Once when he was on his way to the Forest, he recalled, a bolt of lightning missed him by 12 inches.

He also reminisced about the day in 1954 when his mom (Helen Beatty) took him to Yankee Stadium. He saw his idol, Mickey Mantle.

"My mom lived to be 70. On the day she passed, she'd been quiet. Then she had a heart attack. Her idol, Bing Crosby, died the same day: October 14, 1977.

"My dad (Robert Beatty) lived to be about 80. He was feisty, like Teddy Roosevelt. But he'd never put anybody down. He told me, 'Donny, they're all God's children.'"

Beatty is grateful every day he awakens. "If I feel bad, there's somebody out there who feels worse. If my feet get sore, I look at an amputee from war.

"It's a philosophy of staying positive. Get out and try. Even if at first you don't succeed, try and try. The thing that keeps me going is I don't give up."

45

Everybody Loves a Clown: Hy Katz Still Makes 'Em Laugh

(January 18, 2009)

WHEN YOU KNOCK ON HY KATZ' FRONT DOOR, YOU'LL PROBABLY HEAR this shouted from within: "I gave at the office!"

The guy can't help it. He was put on this earth 75 years ago, he will tell you, "To cheer people up."

He did this from behind the grill at Hy's Village Restaurant in Westville for 25 years until 1991. His non-stop eggs and jokes kept his customers entertained and coming back for more.

I spent many amusing mornings at that counter when I lived in Westville. In the rare moments when Katz wasn't cracking a joke, you could read the slogans on his wall. For instance: "Be a regular guy—eat prunes."

Recently I looked up the story I wrote about the sad day he closed down Hy's. The accompanying photo showed a smiling Katz, wearing a shirt that read, "I have the right to be grumpy."

I don't think Katz has been grumpy a day in his life. I've never seen a hint of it in him.

Since selling the restaurant, he has concentrated on his true passion: clowning for kids.

Forty years ago Katz joined the Pyramid Shriners of Milford and signed on to their clown brigade. His first parade was in New Haven, St. Patrick's Day.

He always makes quite an impression with his two-foot-long shoes and large glasses, which earned him the nickname "Big Eyes."

The walls of his Westville home are covered with photos of his clowning exploits. He showed me a sequence from the National Kidney Foundation transplant games, held every two years in cities across the country. Starting in 1998 and continuing through 2008, Katz posed with a sweet-looking kid named Megan, who had received a liver transplant.

Hy Katz. (*New Haven Register* photographer Peter Hvizdak)

"I'll be at the games in 2010 in Wisconsin and I hope she will too," Katz said. "My wife Karol makes all my costumes. She's going to make me a cheese costume for that one."

Although Katz clearly loves being a clown, he said, "Some of the things you see, you're crying underneath. One time we were at a camp for kids with burns. We saw kids with all those scars but they had a beautiful optimism."

Then he remembered a girl at a hospital in Montreal. "She had no arms and no legs but she wanted to blow up a balloon. You see a lot of things. It ain't easy."

When I asked him why he sacrifices so much of his time for clown activities, he of course answered, "To cheer people up."

I asked if he does tricks. He replied, "I can do magic. I walk down the street and I turn into a bar."

Katz spent most of his early years in New London, where his dad, Sam Katz, ran a luncheonette.

"He had a good little business. I was only a kid when I helped out there. The customers were really nice: police department people, Electric Boat workers."

But when Hy was just 10, his dad died. He and his mother, Rose, moved to the Legion Avenue neighborhood of New Haven.

When I suggested he had recreated his dad's place in Westville, Katz nodded.

"You greet people, you call them by name, treat them well and they'll come back," he noted.

He said he closed the restaurant after all those years of getting up at 2:30 a.m. six days a week because his wife was afraid he was going to have a heart attack. But then he confided the real reason he hung up his apron was that the long hours of standing by the grill were killing his feet.

He went on to a succession of morning short-order cook jobs, working for other people. But one by one the places closed, including his most recent gig at a canteen in North Haven.

"There's nothing around," he said. "It's a tough economy."

And so where does Katz spend his mornings now? At McDonald's, the one on Whalley Avenue in Westville. He goes there to eat breakfast with a half-dozen buddies.

After breakfast and working out at the Jewish Community Center, he said, "I'm home, on my own." Clearly, he doesn't like that.

Katz is always up for a clowning event but he told me it's getting harder to assemble his clown buddies. "A lot of the other clowns are gone now," said Katz.

He also noted that not many new clowns are coming up to replace those who have departed.

Things were getting a tad uncheery, so Katz showed me his collection of doll figures and danced along with one after he wound it up. Then he showed me the pet skunk on his mantelpiece; it made an odd, rude noise when Katz pushed a button.

Before I left Hy's funhouse, my old buddy handed me a smile button and a card that read: "This is a free ticket. It's not good for anything. It's just free."

46

The High and the Humble Bid Farewell to City's Iconic Clark's Dairy

(May 28, 2010)

OVER THE PAST SEVERAL WEEKS, AFTER I HAD THE SAD TASK OF BREAK-ing the news to the Elm City community that Clark's Dairy will close Sunday, I have been staring at the "Wall of Fame" in the old place while consuming my scrambled eggs, wheat toast and coffee.

Up on that wall are many famous faces with their tributes to Clark's and its staff. I think the best inscription is that of U.S. Representative Rosa DeLauro, D-3., a longtime New Havener.

This is what she wrote: "To the gang at Clark's, my second home—what would I do without you? Clark's is a special place and you are special people. I treasure your friendship."

Near DeLauro's photo is a framed shot of a fun couple: Bill and Hillary Clinton. When they were dating at Yale Law School in the early '70s, they were known to stop at Clark's. Hillary still raves about the milkshakes.

I wish I'd had a chance to sidle up to the former president when he spoke last Sunday for Yale's Class Day. I would have told him: "Clark's is closing. This is your last chance. Get over there."

During his speech, Clinton reminisced about those law school years. He said he is especially grateful he went to Yale because it was there he met Hillary.

But he noted wistfully, "We've been gone from here since 1973."

He also told the Yale seniors, entering an accelerating world: "Change is hard."

Yes, and the change at Clark's will be very hard to accept.

My time at Clark's goes back almost as far as that of the Clintons, to January 1977, when I arrived in New Haven as a cub reporter. I set up my "Yankee shrine" bachelor pad in a first-floor apartment on Trumbull Street, just around the corner from Clark's.

What a discovery! Between Clark's and the Lincoln Theater, I was in heavenly hands.

As a newcomer to the big city, initially with few friends here, I had many breakfasts, lunches and dinners at Clark's. I was seeking a friendly place to hang out, a long counter where I could converse with the regulars.

Anthony Mihalakos, who with his brother John bought the restaurant from the Clark family in 1962, was always running around behind the counter, serving plates and scooping ice cream. After he suffered a stroke nearly three years ago, it got harder for the dairy to continue.

But in 1977, he was in his prime. Mary Hying was there, too, of course, waiting on the tables and counter. She is a motherly sort, always with a kind word and an interesting piece of local news.

When I began dating my future bride, I introduced her to Clark's. Mary took care of us.

After we got married and had kids, we knew where to bring them. Mary watched them grow.

They're teenagers now, still eating at Clark's Dairy, their food often delivered by Mary. My elder daughter Natalie prefers a Clark's hamburger to those served at Louis' Lunch!

Since I wrote about the Dairy's imminent closing I have heard from locals who remember John Clark and his five Clark's Dairy stores. Irwin (Butch) Brown said his father James Brown was general manager of the stores from the '40s until his death in 1963. James Brown's daughter, Phyllis (Brown) Hunt, offered similar memories.

Bernard Possidente, who worked at several Clark's stores as a busboy and soda jerk, said, "Everyone came to Clark's. The milk bars were places for all ages, young and old, to meet. It was a great night to treat your best girl to Clark's."

And Peggy Saars, 91, called to say that more than 60 years ago her first date with her future husband was at Clark's Dairy. They had an ice cream soda.

What will we do without Clark's Dairy? We'll follow Mary and Clark's Dairy cook Ricky Flores next door to Clark's Pizza and Restaurant, owned by John and Joanna Mihalakos.

The counter is smaller there, but we'll all squeeze in together.

47

Vinny Played Sax. The Five Satins Needed a Solo. The Rest Is History

(December 5, 2010)

For many years Vinny Mazzetta and his wife JoAnn shared only amongst themselves and their family what she called "our little secret."

They instructed their kids not to talk about it with their friends. Nobody would believe it anyway.

But after more than 25 years of secrecy and silence, prodded by his family and seeing yet another story in the *New Haven Register* that overlooked his proper place in history, Mazzetta decided to come out of the closet.

That was me, he publicly stated: I was the one who played saxophone on the Five Satins' "In the Still of the Night," recorded in the basement of St. Bernadette Church.

This is no minor matter. It is one of the most popular, most requested rock 'n' roll songs of all time. You can still hear it played on the radio and at dances. And the sax solo is beautiful.

Now here is my confession, my long-overdue apology: I was one of the reporters who denied Mazzetta his just recognition. My oversight occurred in June 1980.

I spent months tracking down the original members of the Satins. I began by locating Fred Parris, the lead singer and the man who wrote "In the Still of the Night."

Vinny Mazzetta in the basement of St. Bernadette Church. (*New Haven Register* photographer Peter Casolino)

When I asked how they wound up in that church basement in the Morris Cove section of New Haven in February of 1956, Parris told me all of them were broke and needed a free place to record their songs. He said they "made a deal with somebody" who was a parishioner of the church and was "pretty tight with the priest."

This "somebody," Parris said, also played saxophone. The "deal" was that if he could get them in there, they would "let him play sax on the record."

I should have asked Parris: "Who was that saxophone player?" But I didn't, so Mazzetta went uncredited in my big Satins story.

Even after Mazzetta started talking about his role on that song, I still wasn't aware of it. Finally in June 1995, he got recognition when a "Wall of Fame" was created, with plaques, in the church basement.

Mazzetta participated in the ceremony and was shocked that hundreds of people attended. Parris and Mazzetta were reunited, performing that timeless song. Also on hand were Bobby Mapp, the drummer on "Still," and Tom Sokira, who co-produced the record with Marty Kugell.

But alas, I had left New Haven for a couple of years and didn't know it was happening. I was still ignorant about Mazzetta until recently when a neighbor of his called and filled me in.

Last week, I finally met Mazzetta at his home in Morris Cove, where he has remained all these years, less than a mile from that church basement on Townsend Avenue.

He is 75, still energetic, working part-time at a discount store and still playing saxophone informally with friends. He readily agreed to let me drive him to the church where it all happened.

On the way over, I apologized to him for overlooking his place in history. He told me not to worry about it.

When we walked into that basement, a group of school kids were gathered around a piano with their teacher, singing "Rudolph, the Red-Nosed Reindeer." Mazzetta pulled out his saxophone and started playing along with them.

Then I asked if he could play his solo from "In the Still of the Night" and he did so. It's still beautiful. "You hear how good the acoustics are?" he asked. I did.

The plaque on the wall states: "'In the Still of the Night,' the classic rock era song by Fred Parris and the Five Satins was recorded here in St. Bernadette's Church basement on February 19, 1956."

When I noted that Mazzetta's name is not on the plaque, symbolic of recognition still being denied him, he said, "That never bothered me. It bothered my family more than it bothered me."

Asked how he came up with his big solo on that song, he said, "It just came out. I did what I felt."

"Who knew?" he said. "Who knew where it was going to go?"

And how much was Mazzetta paid for his part in this classic hit? "I got $42.50. That was the union recording fee. And I had to pay about $40 to join the union, so actually I made nothing!"

But he didn't feel cheated, given the way record companies deprived most singers and musicians in those days.

Mazzetta never became a member of the Five Satins. He noted they were a vocal group and often used local musicians in the towns where they toured.

But he is proud of what he set in motion; that recording also marked a breakthrough in race relations. "It was a first. You could tell I was only 21. I didn't know any better: bringing blacks into the Cove, into a church. But I just said, 'They're here to make a record.'

"A good thing happened," he said.

48

Here's the Full, Final Story of the Man in the Yellow House

(January 30, 2011)

My neighbors knew him as "the man in the yellow house." Others who knew him better called him "Harry Hero."

His real name was Herbert "Bud" Barker and he packed many memorable moments into a remarkable 89 years.

When I first wrote about him three years ago ("Let me tell you about a bright yellow house on the street where I live"), I drew many details from an email message sent around my East Rock neighborhood by Barker's daughter, Christine Barker.

She wanted us to know about the elderly gentleman we occasionally glimpsed being helped into a van for his daily ride to the Partnerships Center for Adult Day Care in Hamden.

She was correct in thinking we were wondering about him. What was his story?

Barker framed her message as "my quiet request that we all remind ourselves of the true meaning of good neighbors and the joys of diversity."

"The man who lives in the bright yellow house is a World War II veteran," she said. "He is suffering from dementia, which the VA has attributed to multiple head injuries sustained when he was wounded repeatedly during the war."

She noted her father was awarded three Purple Hearts, two Bronze Stars and many other medals.

When Barker was discharged from the U.S. Army, he was classified by the VA as 75 percent disabled. This entitled him to receive regular monthly income benefits for the rest of his life.

But Barker fought this classification, believing he didn't need the benefits. He said they should go to others who needed them more.

The Army lowered his disability ranking to 50 percent. Barker kept asking them to lower it even further but the Army wouldn't do it.

One of Barker's sons, Michael Barker, told me his dad sustained serious injuries on two occasions during the war. Both times it happened on his birthday.

In the more severe occurrence, Barker suffered head wounds and then, along with another American soldier, held 40 German soldiers captive overnight as the Germans sat in a trench.

But Barker, a modest man, was more inclined to reminisce about the time he spent as General George Patton's personal driver along the front lines in France.

Michael Barker noted that when his father began experiencing the early stages of dementia in 1986, doctors said it came from that wartime head injury.

"Basically, he finally succumbed to his wounds," the son told me.

In that neighborhood email message, Christine Barker said that after her father got the diagnosis, he agreed to move from New Jersey to Connecticut with his wife Anne, to be close to other family members.

"He reluctantly and with a great deal of embarrassment admitted to his family his fear of being lost and not knowing which home was his," she said.

He made three requests of his family: paint the house a bright yellow so he would always know which one he should go into; take good care of his wife; and try to keep them together in that yellow house.

The family worked hard and complied with all three of those requests.

Michael Barker noted his father was more than a war hero. After the war he had a law enforcement career with the New York Central Railroad, Penn Central Railroad, Conrail and Metro-North. He became chief of police for Conrail's northeast division and hired the first black officers in two of his departments.

Now here's the "Harry Hero" part. Barker repeatedly helped people in emergencies, the most memorable being the time he saw a car crash on a New York City highway.

"The woman in the car had her skull split open," Michael Barker said. "He ran into the traffic and started treating her. He held her head together."

Not only did the woman survive, but her mental faculties were intact, thanks to "Harry Hero."

On Sunday, January 23 at 12:05 a.m., Christine sent out another email message to the neighborhood.

"For those of you who remember my story of your neighbor, the man in the bright yellow house, I bring you a sad update," she wrote. "That man, my father, Herbert A. Barker, died peacefully in my arms tonight after sharing the day with his wife of 65 years, Anne."

She thanked all of her neighbors who "graciously went out of your way these last few years to say hello and share a moment and smile with him."

I will miss seeing my old neighbor in that bright yellow house. It was a comfort just knowing he was there. But I'm glad that this time, with his family's permission, I can tell you his name and more about his wonderful life.

49

A Family Celebrates 40 Years of Good Times at the Picture Show

(May 15, 2011)

FORTY YEARS AGO THIS WEEK, 15-YEAR-OLD STUART SOFFER AND HIS brother Alan stood in the back of their dad's new venture, the "Mini-Cine," on its opening night, hoping it would all hang together.

"I was very nervous," Stuart recalled. "I thought my dad (Joseph Soffer) was getting involved in a business he knew nothing about."

The movie was "Oliver!," the popular British musical, first released in 1968.

"The theater was full," Stuart noted. "I was so proud. Then the music started and poof! The screen went blank! I was so mortified. Maybe five to 10 seconds later, whoosh, it starts up again!

"Wow! Tears were coming down my eyes. My dad told me, 'This is just my first trial run; what are you crying for? Everything's going to be OK. Don't worry about it.' And the rest of the movie played fine."

Last Thursday night, to commemorate the 40th birthday of the theater, later called Cine 4, the Soffers threw a party for their loyal supporters and employees through the years. The highlight of the party: the brothers again screened "Oliver!"

A few weeks before the anniversary party Stuart told me he was "a little worried" about the technical quality of the film. After all, it's more than 40 years old.

"I've asked for the print to be delivered a week early, so I can screen it in advance, just in case we have to patch up a section or two," Stuart said. "I'll feel a lot better after the screening than I do right now."

He should have heeded the advice from his old man: "Everything's going to be OK. Don't worry about it."

The showing went perfectly. No "poof." I saw Stuart watching from the back of the theater.

Stuart said he and his brother wanted to have the private party as a way to thank a lot of people.

"Forty years!" Stuart exclaimed. "I can't let 40 years go by without a 'thank you' to the people who helped us get by. It took a lot of help over the years to keep this building going.

"It's not a 9-to-5 job," he noted. "People give up their weekends, their holidays. This is for the guy who came in on a Saturday night to make sure we had heat. It's for Louis, who delivered the Cot soda."

But Stuart said it's above all the Soffer family that keeps the place alive. "My brother stands by my side. If I have an event I have to go to, he picks up the slack. And I do the same for him."

When he opened his twin cinema on Middletown Avenue in New Haven, off Exit 8 of Interstate 91, Joseph Soffer might have been a novice in the movie business. But at least he got a chance to establish a toehold and a loyal customer base before the giant multiplexes invaded.

Soffer had a tough time surviving in the 1980s and '90s after Showcase came to North Haven and it was harder for him to get commercial films. But he added two more screens and kept working long hours, assisted by his wife Barbara. Occasionally one of them would make an emergency call to one or both of their sons: "Can you come down and help out?"

Joseph Soffer died in January 2005. But Barbara, who now lives in Florida, came up for the big party. Greeting old friends in the lobby Thursday, she reminisced about opening night: "I was wearing hot pants and boots!"

There were 75 to 100 people milling around Thursday, holding mini-reunions in clusters and sipping wine supplied by Bishop's Orchards Winery.

Stuart had put me on the guest list because I have spent many nights at his theater, not because he wanted publicity. "Leave the pen, the paper, the pictures (photographer), and the work ethic behind. Support the theater with your heart."

So when Lou DeNegre came up to me, introduced himself and told a nice story about what had happened to him at the theater, I couldn't take out my pad and take notes. I asked him to send me an email.

He followed through, writing about his many years of going to "the Mini-Cine," especially enjoying the matinees during school vacations.

"However, the real connection I have is that's where I met my wife," DeNegre said. "It was early 1989 and I went there to pick up a friend who worked there. This friend told me about another girl, Sue, who worked there and who wanted to meet me. We met, went out and got married in 1990."

As the credits rolled on "Oliver!" the crowd burst into applause. I heard somebody say, "They don't make 'em like that anymore!"

Back in the lobby, people were hugging the Soffer brothers and their mom.

"Forty more years, Stu!" I called out to him as I departed.

50

Roger, the Courthouse Greeter, is Still a Man of Mystery

(May 22, 2011)

HE IS A FIGURE I HAVE SEEN ON THE STREETS OF NEW HAVEN, ESPE-cially around the courthouse at Church and Wall Streets, for years.

I have also seen him walking, walking, walking on downtown streets. He is almost always dressed in a fringed leather jacket.

Finally, after asking around, I learned his name: Roger Cruz.

Maryann Ott, a downtown resident who has befriended Cruz, told me some things about him that got me even more interested. She started to fill in some of the blanks. But still there are many unanswered questions.

Ott noted the nice rapport Cruz has with many people in this caring old town.

"There are women who knit him scarves with his name on them, embroider emblems on his jackets and repair his clothes," Ott said. "I don't know who they are but my guess is there are at least eight to 12 women out there looking after him."

Ott also told me, "I think he has a code with himself that he cannot end the day with cash in his pocket. He often buys gifts for his female friends from street vendors. He has given me earrings and necklaces, stones from the Peabody Museum and bracelets."

Ott added, "Instead of doing his laundry, which he hates to do, he throws clothes away and buys new stuff. He has a lawyer who cuts him $50 checks once a week from a fund of some kind."

She also told me, "He had a dog, which he loved, and misses a great deal.

"He worked at Pratt & Whitney at some point but I don't know when or for how long," she said.

And she noted he has a great sense of humor. "I enjoy his company a great deal and like him tremendously."

After hearing from Ott that Cruz goes to Sunday services every week at St. John's Episcopal Church on Humphrey Street, I spoke with a member of the vestry, Lenore Hammers.

"Usually Roger's the first one at the church," she said. "He sits in the back but he likes the socializing. He loves to meet people.

"He goes up for communion and he prays. He sings a little bit, quietly. He always comes to our coffeehouse after the service. He brings in shrimp or cheese or hamburger meat. Whatever he has, he shares.

"He's really sweet," Hammers added. "We like having him in the church."

When I at last introduced myself to Cruz one day on the courthouse steps, I used Ott's name as a starting point. He smiled and nodded.

I know he lives at a subsidized apartment on Park Street, so I asked him about that. "It's a nice place," he said. "I have a nice room."

He told me he's 57 and was born in New Haven. After he finished fifth grade, his family moved to North Branford, where he went to junior high and high school.

"I did graduate high school," he said proudly. "That's the one thing I did."

When I asked if he'd ever considered going to college, he grimaced and said, "It's hard for me to get started."

He left North Branford 30–35 years ago. "My mother was sick. She was driving me nuts. I had to get out of there."

While we sat on the courthouse steps, Cruz periodically called out to a cop, an attorney, a judicial marshal and plenty of other passers-by. "How was your bachelor's party?" he asked a lawyer, who smiled and said it went fine.

Often the people Cruz greets give him a coin or a dollar. But he rarely asks for it. He has never asked me for anything. Nor will he accept my offers for rides, saying he prefers to walk.

Cruz confided he receives medication for his anxiety every morning from a nurse.

"My mind depression takes up all my energy," he said sadly. "I don't know, I call it depression. I can't function."

When I asked if he had a happy childhood, he held his head and said, "I really don't want to get into it."

But he did say, "Back in the day, I got married. That was a damn mistake. Fourteen years. I'm happy to be rid of her. Now I don't have to answer to nobody. I like it like that."

He said he has three kids but hasn't seen them in years. "I hope they're OK."

Cruz also revealed he has a sister in Florida who sends him money periodically. "You need a microscope to see it."

Cruz and I have had a series of conversations over the past few weeks. He always apologizes for not remembering the story from his past he wants to tell me. "My mind is blank," he says.

The saddest thing he told me: when I asked what he does on Saturdays, he said, "I walk around the city, hating myself." I asked why and he replied, "Because I have to come out here to bum money, that's why."

51

New Haven Icon Cutler's Departure a Sign of the Times

(May 18, 2012)

WHEN I GOT THE CALL FROM PHIL CUTLER WEDNESDAY MORNING, THE one I had long dreaded, he kept telling me, "This isn't sad."

He has decided to close Cutler's Record Shop.

Putting a good spin on things, a fitting approach for a man who has spent his life selling records and other discs, Cutler told me this will be a "celebration" of the store's history.

I very much appreciate that history, the great memories and all the years of service by Cutler and his staff. But as a longtime and present-day customer, I am sad. I don't feel like celebrating.

Cutler, an old friend of mine and fellow soccer dad, did admit: "It's like the death of a family member. Maybe it hasn't hit me yet."

When I went down to New Haven's Broadway Wednesday afternoon to do the end-of-Cutler's interview, we sat together and reflected on the other neighborhood institutions on that strip that have departed: the Yankee Doodle Coffee shop, the York Square Cinemas, Elliot Brause's Quality Wine Shop.

Cutler said when Yale alumni come back to town this year for their reunions, they will notice the swan song of Cutler's with sorrow, as will anybody who has spent time in New Haven and returns for a visit. (They'll have until June 30 to stock up on Cutler's bargains.)

Walk down Broadway now and you'll see Urban Outfitters and the Apple Store, but fewer and fewer independent businesses.

We're losing our bookstores and our record stores, the places where we can walk inside and browse, leafing through the selections. I guess now we're supposed to do all that on our computers in solitude.

"The Internet is killing everything," Cutler told me.

Sure, I've got that home computer and I could sit there ordering CDs online. But I very rarely do it. I much prefer going down to Cutler's, chatting with Cutler and his staffers Bob Briar, Mindy Peterman and Kyle Mullins.

I was talking to some of my younger work colleagues about this shopping technique of mine and they didn't seem to get it. Maybe it sounds too leisurely.

But ever since I got to this town in 1977, I've been buying records and then cassettes and then CDs at Cutler's. Last week I was in there ordering a CD of "Neil Young Unplugged."

Obviously there aren't nearly enough people who have my shopping habit.

Cutler will still have a place to go on Broadway; he's overseeing production work at the merchandiser and manufacturer Campus Customs. He was considerate to help Briar and Peterman get jobs there too.

Indeed, when Cutler and I had our interview Wednesday, we spoke at a conference room of Campus Customs. As we entered the building he gestured at a large warehouse room and said, "This is where York Square Cinemas used to be."

And so now Cutler and his former staff will be doing Campus Customs work instead of selling records, in a place that no longer shows movies.

What about the Cutler's mascot cat, Wally? Where will he live now?

"The cat is a problem," Cutler said. "He's such a good boy. People have come in and said they'll take him. But until I'm 100 percent comfortable with it, I can't let him go."

And as for the gigantic blue and yellow phonograph sign that fronted Cutler's until the store was downsized in 1999, Cutler said it's in storage. He's entertaining ideas on what to do with it.

Clearly, Cutler is torn about this closing. He said there was unending daily pressure keeping the place going; he started working in the family store with his dad Jayson at age 13.

"I loved every day," he told me. "It wasn't a job; it was a lifestyle."

Although he went to college for a couple of years, "all I wanted to do was be in that store." So he came home.

"The whole thing was a blessing," he said. "I saw a great opportunity and I ran with it."

We're lucky we were able to run along with him for so many years.

52

He Had a Great Run and He Did it His Way, that Ol' "Doc" Whitney

(February 24, 2013)

IN A RARE DEPARTURE FROM HIS EVER-UPBEAT DEMEANOR, "Doc" George Whitney once told me, as he alluded to the death of his wife Dorothy, "None of us can go on forever."

But it seemed to many people who knew him that somehow, he could.

Even when I received a dire-sounding email message from Whitney's daughter Carolyn Sabol last Monday, reporting he had become seriously ill and Hospice staffers had been called in, I couldn't really believe it.

The last time I saw him, on New Year's Day during our annual get-together at Orange's Chilly Chili 5-kilometer road race, he was as spry and chipper as ever.

He was wearing a white shirt with "94" on the back in honor of his age. And of course he had on that bright orange beanie and mismatched socks.

He enjoyed telling people why he didn't wear matching socks. The subject came up one day in January 2008 when I was interviewing him at his home in Orange, with Dorothy sitting nearby. She pointed out his "peculiarity" and I proceeded to notice one of his socks was yellow and one was pink.

"Too much time is spent sorting out clean socks," he told me with a grin.

George "Doc" Whitney outside his home in Orange. (*New Haven Register* photographer Brad Horrigan)

And so as a tribute to him I always wore mismatched socks when I ran in the Chilly Chili. I also wore mismatched socks all of this past week in the hope that it might help him to pull through this spot of bother.

But on Thursday night, Sabol sent me another email. That afternoon, with his family gathered around his bed in the family's home in Brattleboro, Vermont, the great man's heart had stopped beating.

She said he had fallen during a run, February 2, and cut his eye. It healed but it took something out of him. Shortly afterward he developed an infection and seemed to lose his will to live.

He had fallen before, at the Chilly Chili race January 1, 2012. But even a trip to the hospital that day didn't dampen his effervescence.

Sure, he was embarrassed, and very disappointed that he had failed to finish the race after tripping and going down about a half-mile from the finish line. Because he hit his head on the pavement, medics insisted he climb into an ambulance and get checked out at the hospital.

I was waiting at the finish line for him when I heard he had fallen. I decided to go to Yale-New Haven Hospital to see how he was doing.

After about an hour, his daughter Kate Consiglio came out to the waiting room. She was smiling and wearing his orange beanie.

She reported he just had a bruise over his eye and needed a few stitches.

"He's mad," she told me. "He said, 'They took my socks off! Why'd they take my socks off?'"

Back home in Vermont a few days later, he sent me a cheery email message. Summing up his hospital experience, he said, "I had an interesting and happy time. How can all that misery be recalled with so much happiness?"

That was classic "Doc" Whitney.

Last month he made it to that finish line. He had to pause a bit on the last stretch and when I saw him at the end he was rueful. "I ran out of gas!" he told me.

But then he smiled and jogged off to get some chili. My parting sight of him was enjoying a bowl, surrounded by friends and well-wishers.

He was an inspiration to me and many other runners. Seeing his example, we believe we can keep going too, well down that road.

But he was more than just a dedicated runner. He had one of the liveliest minds I've ever come across.

When I spoke with him at his farm in Orange in 2008, where for many years he had worked as a veterinarian specializing in treating small animals such as reptiles and birds, he was talking about a 93-page book he had written. He entitled it "A Time For Action."

He was calling for the elimination of lobbyists. He asked: "Why not create a voluntary pledge to present to a legislator, present or aspiring, to take if he or she wants my vote? A pledge that states, 'If I win the election, neither I nor my staff will have anything personal to do with lobbyists.'"

He noted a friend had told him, "George, that's pie in the sky."

"Well, every idea is pie in the sky," Whitney replied. "If it's worth anything, it'll fly. If it's not, it'll die."

He told me: "If we get enough people to take the pledge, it could be a powerful tool. It could change the whole government."

Yes, even at age 89, "Doc" Whitney believed he could change the world.

I will close with some of my favorite sayings from the back of my "I am a 'Doc' Whitney wannabee" running shirt:

"No, I'm not on steroids but thanks for asking."

"Mother told me never to associate with fast women."

"I intend to run forever. So far, so good."

53

Recalling Eddie Malone and the Famed Three Steins Grille

(May 17, 2013)

WHEN THE NEWS CAME THAT JAMES EDWARD MALONE HAD DIED LAST week at age 90, I thought back to a wildly sentimental gathering: the night we closed Malone's Three Steins Grille.

Malone's son Michael, who was there that night in May 1979 with his family, told me Wednesday: "Everybody walked away with something." He meant we all left with a piece of the place.

Sometime after midnight Eddie Malone ("Nobody called him 'James,'" Michael noted) climbed atop a stool and began pulling out pieces of the wall, flinging fragments into the rowdy crowd.

We were shouting "Eddie! Eddie!" and then serenaded him with a chorus of "For He's a Jolly Good Fellow," according to my cub reporter's write-up.

I'll bet my notebook was stained with beer and sweat, and that some of my jottings were incomprehensible.

Nine hours before he started dismantling his basement joint on Church Street near the corner of Grove, Malone sat at the bar and reminisced.

"There are 46 years here, 46 years of tradition," he told me, alluding to the bar-restaurant's beginning in 1933 in the hands of his dad, James Edward Malone Sr. "You can't duplicate that with a million dollars.

"It's the warmth of the place that brings people here, and the warmth of the customers. We're moving out of our home."

Malone was being forced to move, to relocate around the corner at the former Seven Gables, because the building's owner had made a financial decision.

Malone termed it "a question of economics." He noted, "Everything changes."

His son, who worked at the Three Steins as a busboy, then a bartender, called it "a great melting pot of people."

Asked what he can recall of that final night, he said, "I just remember a lot of people coming down for it: judges, attorneys, SNET (Southern New England Telephone) executives, construction workers, students. People from all walks of life."

The closing might have been even crazier than the St. Patrick's Day galas there. "The parade ended on that corner," Michael said. "So everybody would come down (the Malone's stairs) and celebrate."

Eddie Malone was always the big draw. "My father was a very social person. He spoke to everybody. He liked to laugh and joke and tell stories. People sometimes told me he was like a second father to them."

The second Malone's had its run from 1979 to 1988, according to Michael. It was forced to close when the building was torn down to make way for the Century, a multi-story office complex.

From there, Eddie Malone went to State Street to operate yet another Malone's until 1996. Then he finally retired.

Although Malone had grown tired of the daily bar-managing demands, he hated being at home, away from all those people downtown. And so eventually he took a job as "host" at Tycoon's, a bar-restaurant across from the New Haven Coliseum before that fabled arena also was demolished.

Malone received a military funeral Monday, with a 21-gun salute, two Marines on duty and the playing of "Taps." The Marines presented his wife Kathryn with an American flag.

"My dad was a true patriot," Michael said. He told me his father left Wesleyan University to join the Marine Corps and serve in World War II. He was a mortar crewman at the Battle of Iwo Jima.

But when he came home and got his Wesleyan degree, Malone did not care to talk about his war experiences. He didn't even allow a gun to be in his house.

Michael said Three Steins was "absolutely" the best of his dad's bars. "It wasn't the same in the other places. It'd be like if they built a new Fenway Park."

As for the bar scene in New Haven today, Michael said, "There's nothing quite like Three Steins."

54

Now the Leader of the Pack is Gone, Never to Sing Again

(May 24, 2013)

IT WASN'T SO LONG AGO, JUST LAST SEPTEMBER, THAT WE WERE CEL-ebrating with Ann DeMatteo at the Karaoke Heroes club downtown because she had been promoted to managing editor of one of our affiliates, the Middletown Press.

That night she and I decided to reprise our performance of "The Leader of the Pack," the classic Shangri-Las motorcycle love story, which we had done three decades earlier during a wild *New Haven Register* party in "The Passion Pit," reporter Eddie Petraiuolo's basement apartment on Livingston Street.

That doesn't seem so long ago either. But it was. Young and innocent days.

On Tuesday afternoon, as I stood alongside Ann's casket at the funeral home and said goodbye and thanks for the memories, my mind flashed back to those fun-filled days and nights.

We thought they would never end. We believed we would all go on spending Friday afternoons together at Rice Field in East Rock Park, playing softball ("beerball," actually) after work, then staggering over to Archie Moore's for pitchers at happy hour.

Happy together we all were.

Ann DeMatteo. (*New Haven Register* file photo)

Life intrudes. Within only a few years Eddie Petraiuolo, the robust and invincible, my best buddy and a good friend of Ann's, would contract throat cancer and die, at age 28.

And 24 years after Eddie left us, Kathy Kemp, who danced and sang with us in "The Pit," knowing every word of the Supremes' "Stop! In the Name of Love," as did Ann, would be dead of breast cancer.

And now Ann has been felled by the same disease, after such a gallant and inspirational resistance.

What a performer! On the day she got married in 1982, the reception was held at a big hall, big enough for all of us to dance. And because it was the day before Halloween, we put on masks and gyrated to "The Monster Mash."

Ann led the charge. She always got people dancing with her.

Three months ago, when it really seemed Ann was dying, many of us gathered around her bed at the hospital. We thought we were saying goodbye. Again, we had underestimated her.

But there we all were, so I told the story about trying to get Meat Loaf's "Paradise by the Dashboard Light" at Karaoke Heroes so she and I could really cut loose and her theatrical spirit could soar. But that song, apparently too long, was not on the playlist.

And so we settled for our theme song, "Leader of the Pack." It was a crowd-pleaser, just as it had been all those years ago.

When I recalled this as I stood by Ann's bed, she smiled, but she was having trouble talking. She waved at me.

Then she found the strength and courage to hold on for three more months. Amazing.

How can I not now think about all of us dancing together at Eddie's place?

Life is a lottery, folks. Some of us are lucky; some are not.

No, life isn't fair.

And so I never got to do "Paradise" with Ann. It would've been a big hoot.

But instead Miss Ann DeMatteo has joined Eddie Petraiuolo in that great record hop in the sky.

55

The Delight of Having a Typewriter
Repairman as a Friend

(August 30, 2013)

IN MARCH 1989, NEARLY A QUARTER OF A CENTURY AGO, I STOPPED IN at Manson Whitlock's typewriter shop, which was then on the ground floor of 276 York Street, to interview him for the Yale Alumni Magazine.

I didn't realize it at the time but this gentle, warm man would become my most unforgettable character and a friend and father figure, as well as a story subject.

He died Wednesday at his home in Bethany at age 96, only two months after having to close his shop because a kidney ailment forced him to go to the hospital.

We won't see anyone like him again.

During my visit with him on that long-ago day in March, he sat at his desk amidst assorted typewriter parts, working on an old Underwood manual model. A bust of Mark Twain watched over him nearby.

Every few minutes Whitlock reached into his tobacco pouch to refill his pipe. Meanwhile, he tossed off funny, self-deprecating remarks about his life's business.

Already at that time, some Yale students and professors were making the switch to computers. But he told me, "I think they'll ruin everyone's brains. People don't have to think anymore to work out things. They push buttons and the answer comes out."

Whitlock took a quiet pride in his work. He had plenty of famous customers but he said, "I'm not going to get into personalities and name-dropping."

Then he fiddled with his tobacco pouch, grinned shyly and confided, "I'll bet Gerald Ford would admit to being in Whitlock's at one time."

He also let me know that Yale President A. Bartlett Giamatti bought a typewriter from him. "A Smith-Corona, as I recall."

When I broached the idea of retirement, Whitlock, then in his early 70s, said, "I've got to stay busy, that's for sure. I've been here for 54 years now and I don't think I'm good for many more." (Ha!)

Manson Whitlock in his typewriter shop. (*New Haven Register* photographer Jeff Holt)

He noted his wife Nancy was very ill. She would die seven years later, prompting him to tell me he had "lost interest in living." But that wasn't true either.

In 1990, I interviewed him again, when the rising rent and those infernal onrushing computers caused him to prepare to close that office. Again he talked of retirement but he said he didn't want to lose touch with his friends and customers. And so he moved up to the second floor, where he made his long, final stand.

Through the 1990s and the past decade, I came to know him as a buddy while providing you readers with updates on how he was doing up there.

When I learned his birthday was February 21, I began a custom of bringing him a cupcake every year on that date. He was a sweet guy with a sweet tooth; I knew he always looked forward to my arrival with that treat.

During one of my visits he presented me with a beautiful old Underwood he had restored. It sits in my office at home.

Over the past year, I noticed he was slowing down. When I saw him last December he said, "The stairs get steeper and steeper." He said he was accepting fewer customers.

But still he made that morning drive in from Bethany, rarely missing a day's work. He was proud of his driving ability, often reminding me he had spent 80 years on the road "without a smirch on my license."

On February 21 of this year, his 96th birthday, he greeted me warmly as always and enjoyed the cupcake. But he confessed, "My brain, eyes and fingers don't work as well together as before."

When I left his office that day, he told me, "I have an appointment one year from today for another cupcake—the Lord willin' and the creek don't rise!"

But the creek did rise. That was our last cupcake.

As a way to encapsulate what Manson Whitlock meant to me and so many others, I'll harken back to what he told me all those years ago in 1989 as he contemplated his cluttered workplace: "I've never been a businessman. I never made much money. But I have performed a needed service for a lot of people for a lot of years."

56

Savoring a Long, Romantic Life of Pleasurable Work

(June 22, 2014)

ON A MOMENTOUS JUNE DAY 50 YEARS AGO, JOSEPH ST. JOHN, OWNER OF The Owl Shop in downtown New Haven, approached an enthusiastic young customer named Joe Lentine and told him, "It's about time you started working here."

"I didn't have a summer job," Lentine noted as he recalled this event. "So I said, 'OK. When do I start?'"

"Tomorrow," St. John replied.

Lentine remembered: "As I turned to leave, he called me back from the door and said, 'Don't forget to wear a tie.'"

"And the rest is history," Lentine told me with a small, modest smile.

That summer job began a 50-year stretch of employment, a record of steady longevity we rarely see in today's mobile, fast-changing job market.

Consider what the world was like at that time in 1964: the Beatles were still a new cultural phenomenon in America. Lyndon B. Johnson was president, in just his first year in the White House after John F. Kennedy's assassination. And few people were worried about the effects of smoking, let alone second-hand smoke.

At the end of that summer, Lentine, who was only 19, informed St. John he had to leave The Owl Shop to resume his study of Spanish literature at what was then Southern Connecticut State College. St. John reluctantly watched him go, but called him back to work that Christmas season.

Lentine kept coming back every summer and Christmas until he got his undergraduate and master's degrees, both in Spanish literature.

In 1968, knowing Lentine was done with his schooling, St. John said, "I need you full-time."

Lentine accepted without hesitation. "I could never figure out what I wanted to do anyway," he noted. "I could have taught Spanish. But the language of cigars is Spanish—and they don't talk back."

I first met Lentine in 1990, when he was a relative newcomer to The Owl Shop and I was writing about the place as a freelancer for the Yale Alumni Magazine. At that time he told me: "We do things the old way here. Our philosophy is, 'If it's working, don't mess with it.'"

St. John had died by then but his wife Catherine St. John was capably overseeing the shop. She told me then how her husband had opened his first store in 1934 on Wall Street in New Haven. He sold books, typewriters, stationery, shoes and yes, tobacco. He mixed his own blends of it.

The St. Johns expanded in the 1930s and '40s, operating five stores at their peak time. But in 1951, they consolidated, buying the building on College Street next to another downtown mainstay, The Anchor bar and restaurant.

"You know what I figured out today?" Lentine mused when I visited him last week. "I've been here longer than anybody, including Mr. St. John."

Catherine St. John also is deceased. In 1998, the shop was sold to a local neurosurgeon, Dr. Alvin Greenberg. A few years later his son Glen Greenberg took it over.

"He wanted to put a bar in here and get a liquor license," Lentine said of Glen Greenberg. He did so in 2006. Lentine said of this innovation: "It's been a phenomenal success."

"But Glen retained the old atmosphere of the place," Lentine said. "It's been a delight to work for him as well as the St. Johns."

Greenberg's idea also turned out to be a shrewd business move. Because he had an existing tobacco store and obtained the liquor license before the state passed a law prohibiting smoking inside such public

Joe Lentine at The Owl Shop. (*New Haven Register* photographer Peter Hvizdak)

places, The Owl Shop's customers can still enjoy their cigars, pipes or cigarettes while drinking or just relaxing in the cigar lounge.

Indeed, when I stopped in there last Thursday afternoon it had the air of a men's lounge. Several gents were ensconced in leather chairs. They smiled as they puffed away on their cigars.

Greenberg also bestowed upon Lentine the title of master tobacconist.

"I think it's a bit grandiose," Lentine said. "But I can live with it. Mr. St. John was a true master tobacconist. He taught me everything I know."

Lentine still spends part of his workdays mixing the tobacco, a hand-blending process. He also orders the tobacco products, handles mail orders, and waits on customers.

"I love what I do," he said. "I like to help people choose a cigar that will be pleasing to them."

When Jesse Horsford of North Haven paused by the front cigar case to ponder his options, Lentine was there to assist and advise.

"That looks good," Horsford eventually decided. He selected two of the Davidoff Anniversarios, No. 3.

"I think this place is great," Horsford told me. "Joe is very knowledgeable. He always suggests good cigars. I don't think you can do better."

When I asked Lentine if he has ever questioned his decision to remain at The Owl Shop for so long, he said, "At times I regretted it. But yesterday is history. I don't think it's good to dwell on it.

"I'm here with people who have similar interests but from all walks of life," he noted. "And I love being around Yale."

He said he never knows what kind of person might walk in. "You get an electrician, a doctor; everybody's equal when they're smoking a cigar. It makes for a very convivial atmosphere."

He reeled off the names and preferences of past Yale presidents, including Kingman Brewster Jr. (Danish cigarillo) and A. Bartlett Giamatti (W.B. No. 3 pipe tobacco).

When playwright Athol Fugard walked in recently after being away for many years, Lentine astounded him by calling out: "Mr. Fugard! I've got your Mystique tobacco."

Lentine said cigar smoking remains "one of life's little pleasures" despite the warnings of doctors and anti-smoking activists.

He said his health is still good. "I smoke one cigar a day, sometimes two. I abide by Aristotle's golden rule: 'Moderation in everything.'"

Lentine has never married, "but that's not by choice. I'm probably way too fussy."

Still, he said, "I think tobacco is very romantic."

57

"The Movie Man" Lived and Died as a Free Spirit

(March 1, 2015)

BOB PAGLIA, KNOWN TO MANY AS "THE MOVIE MAN," HAD ALWAYS seemed ageless, indestructible and almost as immortal as Count Dracula, the film character Paglia admired and masqueraded as on many occasions.

But a week and-a-half ago, his free-wheeling, rugged and eccentric lifestyle—living in his car, hanging out in diners and Dunkin' Dounts late into the night, refusing to see a doctor—finally caught up with him. "He fell twice in a bank parking lot in Westville," said his long-time friend Elizabeth Walker. "He was lying down but still trying to get people to go away."

An ambulance was called in. Paglia died at the hospital.

"Maybe it was pneumonia," Walker said. "He had signed himself out of the hospital two months ago and seemed to be recovering."

People who knew Paglia had noticed a bulge in his abdomen over the past year but he seemed unconcerned.

"It was a hernia," Walker said, "that grew and grew into the size of a basketball."

When I asked Walker why Paglia loathed doctors and hospitals, she said, "His mother and father both died in a hospital. And the people weren't nice to him when he was there. They ordered him around. He wouldn't put himself at the mercy of that type of people."

Bob Paglia, "The Movie Man." (*New Haven Register* photographer Peter Casolino)

Paglia always did everything on his own terms. He couldn't bear to live any other way.

When I interviewed him 11 years ago for a column, he described himself as "a lone wolf."

He refused to tell me his age. "Just say I'm an archetype." But Walker said after Paglia died that he had made it to 68.

Paglia told me that when he was a boy in Hamden he often walked four miles to New Haven's downtown movie theaters to feast on cowboy fare and his favorite horror films. In addition to the original "Dracula," starring Bela Lugosi, these included "King Kong" and "Frankenstein" (Boris Karloff).

In 1977, he answered an ad placed by WELI radio. "Wanted: movie critic."

He got the job and became "The Movie Man." After reviewing movies on WELI for nearly 20 years, he was forced to leave because of a corporate changeover. But he landed a volunteer movie gig at Citizens Television, the New Haven-based public access cable station. He continued to do reviews there up until his death.

Maybe you saw him on TV. Once you did, you could never forget it. He always wore a big black gaucho hat (even indoors) and leather or black denim clothes. During his show he kept in front of him mascot dolls, including the Count from "Sesame Street."

Every film he reviewed was rated on a precise scale. For instance, when he evaluated "Last Vegas" in 2013, he said, "You'll laugh and you'll be emotionally moved. I give it 3 ½ Paglia paw prints of approval."

That wasn't all he did on CTV. For a Halloween special he dressed as Dracula, with a black cape and fangs. He stalked the CTV hallways, cornering a woman and biting her neck.

For one of his specials, entitled "'The Movie Man' Meets the Son of Howard Hughes," he did a lengthy telephone interview with an odd individual who claimed to be Douglas Hughes, long-lost son of the wealthy tycoon aviator. He said a family member had swindled him out of his inheritance.

Paglia also had a CTV show called "Somatology," which he defined as "a philosophical specialty that focuses on anatomy as a source of all our belief systems and values." (Paglia was very philosophical; he taught that subject at Gateway Community College.)

For many of his "Somatology" shows, Paglia would choose one of his Gateway students—always a woman—to serve as a subject while he demonstrated "the ancient knowledge system of reflexology." Then he massaged her feet.

Walt Bradley, the CTV production manager, said Paglia "was definitely an interesting cat. He was known here on State Street as 'the Count' or 'the Professor.'

"He considered himself 'the poet warrior,'" Bradley noted. "He carried with him Ayn Rand's 'Atlas Shrugged' and books by (the German philosopher) Friedrich Nietzsche and 'TV Guide.' He kept everything in duplicate. He was a pack rat."

Bradley recalled seeing Paglia riding his bicycle through the streets of New Haven and Hamden and even to Orange Showcase Cinemas. On his handlebars he always had large baggies full of stuff. But in recent years, as a concession to the fact that even he was getting older, Paglia had switched to a dented green Plymouth Acclaim (he called it "the Green Hornet"), which he filled with his many possessions.

Bradley often sat down to converse with Paglia. "He'd talk to you about philosophy for hours or about movies—Hopalong Cassidy's pearl-handled gun. He'd give you little glimpses of his life but never anything personal."

Bradley remembered a long time ago seeing Paglia hanging out at the Acropolis Diner in Hamden, "talking to the Turkish cook about Nietzsche."

"Ten years ago we were asking, 'How is this guy still alive?'" Bradley noted. "He willed himself."

When the CPTV people realized Paglia had left his Hamden home and was living out of his car, they tried to help him get lodging. "He was too proud," Bradley said. "He just didn't want to impose on anybody. I don't think he wanted a home."

Walker told me, "He didn't want to be controlled by a landlord or have neighbors bothering him.

"He wasn't staying in his freezing car overnight," she said. "He'd jump from diner to doughnut shop, wherever friendly people would let him sit and read. He was always reading."

In recent years, I sometimes saw Paglia at Books & Company in Hamden, reading with a magnifying glass. Linda Mooser, who owns the store, said he would come in with his bags of books and remain for hours. "He had strong opinions but he was always very mild-mannered."

During one period, before Paglia joined L.A. Fitness in order to have a place to shower and bathe, Mooser noticed he was using her store's bathroom "extensively to wash up. That's when I got the idea he was living in his car. He had so much stuff in it! I was amazed he could fit inside."

Walker told me last Wednesday that Paglia's Plymouth probably was still parked at the bank lot in Westville, so I went to check it out.

And there it was, "the Green Hornet," covered with snow and ice but with many of his possessions still visible—bags of clothing, philosophy books, film tapes ("Superman," "The Dark Night") and notebooks.

Walker said of Paglia, "Romance was his life." But he never married.

"Bob was very courtly," she said. "He had knightly values."

58

Hamden's Native Son Reflects on Age, Sex, Poetry, Baseball

(May 10, 2015)

DONALD HALL SITS ALONE IN HIS GREAT-GRANDFATHER'S HOUSE AT Eagle Pond Farm in Wilmot, New Hampshire, looking out the window at birds, the seasonal changing landscape and the unused barn while thinking about his long life—including old friends in his childhood home of Hamden.

At 86, Hall is still writing. But it's no longer poetry, for which he has won wide acclaim. He was U.S. Poet Laureate from 2006 to 2007.

"As I grew older," he wrote in his recently-published book "Essays After Eighty" (Houghton Mifflin Harcourt), "poetry abandoned me. How could I complain after 70 years of diphthongs? The sound of poems is sensual, even sexual.

"For a male poet," he added, "imagination and tongue-sweetness require a blast of hormones. When testosterone diminishes . . ."

But Hall is not feeling sorry for himself. "I survive into my eighties, writing, and oddly cheerful, although disabled and largely alone," he wrote in one of the essays, "One Road."

He also has his beloved Boston Red Sox to watch on his television set.

"The Red Sox are terrible so far," he acknowledged in an email to me last week. But he added, "I have some hope."

As for my question about the state of his health, he observed, "Every day I am a day older. I feel more tired more often, and take more naps.

"This winter my right knee totally collapsed beneath me twice as I tried to step down from my porch. I waited a while until the firemen rescued me. Each time I was trying to leave the house with somebody else but I was too heavy to raise up.

"I live on one floor, and have for years, and get around decently with a Rollator."

In another of his essays, "Death," he described his daily existence as "spasming from one place to another, pushing a four-wheeled roller. I try not to break my neck. I write letters, I take naps, I write essays."

One of his correspondents is the novelist Alice Mattison, who lives in New Haven. They have been exchanging letters and manuscripts since 1986.

Mattison was a close friend of Hall's wife, also a poet, Jane Kenyon. She died of leukemia in 1995 at age 47. Hall continues to grieve.

"He's a lot like he seems to be on paper," Mattison told me. "Immensely kind and smart. Jane used to say he's good at feeling. He has a tremendous understanding of human emotions. That's what drew Jane to him."

When I remarked to Mattison that Hall sometimes comes across in his essays as a curmudgeon, she said she wouldn't use that word to describe him. "He certainly has strong ideas that he won't change. He believes what he believes and he's not shy about it. But he's not a hard person to get along with at all."

Mattison makes a comical cameo appearance in "Essays After Eighty" when Hall recalls she "twice bopped me on the face to dislodge a Kent."

"Yeah, I hit him a couple of times," Mattison told me. "I didn't know he smoked because he concealed it. Then one day at his mother's house he went outside and he lit up. And I hit him." She said she was justified because of the adverse health effects of smoking.

Mattison noted Hall has never used a computer, a subject he sounded off on in his essay "A House Without a Door." "I inhabit the only computerless home the length of Route 4, and I don't have an iThing. I do have a television set, for MSNBC and baseball. In newspapers and magazines I read about what's happening. Apparently Facebook exists to extinguish friendships. Email and texting destroy the post office. EBay replaces garage sales. Amazon eviscerates bookstores."

Well, so how does he answer my questions via email? He has a devoted and efficient assistant who receives his emails, then prints and delivers them to Hall. He writes out his responses in longhand and she puts them on her computer.

When I asked him if he could imagine ever reading a newspaper online, he replied, "I don't suppose I have ever read anything on a computer, much less a newspaper. I have been holding the news in my two hands every morning for 70-odd years. I should do it another way?"

Donald Hall. (*New Haven Register*; courtesy Houghton Mifflin Harcourt)

Hall said the first newspaper he read was the morning *Journal-Courier* and its sister paper, the *New Haven Register*, circa 1938. He spent his early years living on Ardmore Street in Hamden and attending Spring Glen Grammar School, as it was called in those days.

"Milk arrived every morning from the horse cart of my family's Brock-Hall Dairy," he wrote in his essay "Garlic With Everything." "I walked home from Spring Glen Grammar School at noon for a peanut butter and jelly sandwich."

Hall described that elementary school as "suburban middle class and pale." But when he arrived at Hamden High School, "I first heard 'Paisan!' shouted from one friend to another." Hall discovered second-generation Italians, garlic and pizza, which at that time was "exotic."

Hall wrote that he turned out more and more poetry by age 15 in an effort to appeal to cheerleaders. It didn't work.

But he did attract some notice, at least from the guys, when he became a high school sports correspondent for the *Register* and *Journal-Courier* in 1942.

"I loved working for the *Register* for 10 cents a column inch," Hall told me in an email. "I would come late-late to the *Register* after covering a hockey game between Hamden and Hillhouse. I would sit in the almost-deserted sports department, typing an account of the game, paragraph by paragraph, and the editor would come to the desk, rip out a page and take it down to the typographers."

Hall spent his final high school years at the prep school Phillips Exeter, then went on to Harvard. He and Kenyon, his second wife, moved to New Hampshire in 1975.

In September 2011, six months after President Barack Obama presented Hall with the National Medal of Arts, Hall was surprised to be invited back to his old hometown for a celebration of that medal and his 83rd birthday. In his email to me, Hall wrote he was amazed and ecstatic that 400 people came to Hamden's Miller Memorial Library. After his reading, he recalled, "People surrounded me. 'My mother taught you French!' 'I worked for your father's brother!'"

Hall said Hamden High School held its class reunion during his visit, and so many of his classmates came to the library. "I saw an old girlfriend. Unforgivably, I did not recognize her. I'm pretty sure no one could recognize me, flopping with beard and unruly hair."

In his book of essays Hall wrote that the event in the Hamden library "pleased me as much as the White House."

But in response to my question of whether he will be able to return once more to Hamden, Hall wrote, "I don't think I will ever get back. It is hard to travel. I get tired and uncomfortable if anybody drives me any distance. When I get there, what can I do about steps?"

He said he still has "dear friends" in Spring Glen and would love to see them. But he cannot.

Noting that Hall in his essay referred to elder care institutions as "expiration dormitories" and "storage bins," I nevertheless asked him if he could envision a circumstance in which he would move to such a place. He said he could not but added, "I may have nothing to say about it, if I go totally blooey. No dementia yet! I want to die in the bed where Jane died."

59

A Commitment to a Cemetery
and Each Other

(July 12, 2015)

ON ANY GIVEN DAY OF THE WEEK, IF YOU WALK BENEATH THE ORNATE
entryway of the Grove Street Cemetery (with its inscription "The Dead
Shall Be Raised"), you will see Bill and Joan Cameron in their chapel that
became an office, or out on the grounds of this historic 18-acre expanse.

You might see them answering the phone to sell a grave plot or
attending a funeral to comfort grieving families.

You might even see one of them digging a grave.

"Last fall she dug one," Bill said, nodding affectionately toward his
wife as they sat near each other in their office last Wednesday morning.

"It was a day we were busy with about five funerals," he recalled. "The
next thing you know, she's digging!"

"I took my time," she noted.

"Joan and I have dug graves here in weather beyond description," he
said. "Snow, ice. For years, we didn't have a jackhammer. We used an ax.
(He pointed to the implement, propped up in the corner.) I guess you
could say we didn't know any better. I finally got a jackhammer about
eight years ago."

He is 84; she is 77. But as the superintendents of this unique property,
they're always ready to pitch in to keep the old place going. (They do have
a crew of much younger people to do virtually all the grave-digging.)

For the past 30 years, the Camerons have worked side-by-side, seven days a week, never complaining about that unforgiving commitment.

"I'm here Christmas, New Year's, Easter, every day," he told me. "I put in 70 to 80 hours every week. I don't mind doing it because I grew up in a family business with long hours."

That was Cameron's Restaurant at Savin Rock Amusement Park in West Haven. The fabled park is long gone and so is the restaurant, which Cameron said was forced out by eminent domain.

But one day in 1953, before the eatery closed, Joan walked past and spotted Bill inside. "I kind of made eyes at him."

Shortly afterward, she recalled, "A friend of mine introduced me to Bill. And that was the end of it." She paused to correct herself: "The beginning!"

"And we've been happily married ever since," he said. "That was the best day of my life, the day I met her.

"We got married almost right away," he added. "She lassoed me!

"She's a good person to work with," he noted. "We never have an argument. People tell me, 'If I ever worked with my wife, we'd kill each other!'"

When I asked how they pull it off, she replied, "I'm easy to get along with."

"I am, too," Bill said. "We enjoy being together."

"I don't put in the long hours he does," she noted. "But I do work seven days. I work full-time; he works full-full time."

They come in together at about 6 a.m. She likes to do the bookkeeping then, when it's quiet. By early afternoon she's gone but he stays on.

I asked them when they take vacations. "We don't," he said.

Their employers, the members of the Standing Committee of the Proprietors of the New Haven City Burial Ground (the formal name of the cemetery), are grateful and amazed by the Camerons' dedication.

"They have been marvelous," said Jerry Gaab, the committee's treasurer. "The cemetery has pretty much been their lives. Few people would put in that kind of time."

Gaab wanted to make sure I was aware of how the cemetery was created. I told him I have a booklet outlining the history of the place, published by the committee in 2005.

In 1794, the New Haven Green, which was the city's first common burial site, became too crowded to continue in that capacity. In 1796, a group of citizens, led by U.S. Senator James Hillhouse, laid out the new cemetery on Grove Street, on the border of Prospect Street. Many of the tombstones on the Green were moved to the new site.

The first person to be buried there, on November 9, 1797, was Martha Townsend. Other prominent people since interred there include Hillhouse, Eli Whitney, Noah Webster, 13 Yale presidents, including Kingman Brewster Jr. and A. Bartlett Giamatti; Walter

Bill and Joan Cameron in their office at the Grove Street Cemetery. (*New Haven Register* photographer Peter Hvizdak)

Camp, "the father of American football;" Roger Sherman, who signed the Declaration of Independence and the United States Constitution; and former New Haven Mayor Richard C. Lee.

But one of the prime attractions for the public is the marker of somebody who isn't really buried there: that of Glenn Miller, the bandleader whose plane vanished overseas on December 15, 1944. In December 1998, on the 54th anniversary of his death, a memorial headstone was erected and a memorial service held at the cemetery. The plot and headstone were purchased by Peter Cofrancesco of Hamden.

"That's one of our most asked for," Bill told me. "Eli Whitney and Noah Webster have to take a back seat."

Bill estimated there are nearly 18,000 people buried in the cemetery. He said there is still room for about 500 more. It costs $6,500 to buy a plot, which allows for four cremations. Half-plots are offered for $3,250.

Bill said when he started working at the cemetery in 1976, only about 5 percent of the bodies were cremated. Now it's about 80 percent.

After he put in about seven years, Bill was named superintendent. Within a year or two after that, Joan got tired of "sitting in a dark room all day" for the phone company and joined her husband.

For about 25 years their son William Cameron III worked with them. But four years ago he moved to North Carolina to raise animals on a farm and do landscaping.

When they were younger, the Camerons sometimes talked about moving to the South and owning a farm with pigs. When I asked Joan about that, she said they have no regrets about staying in their West Haven home and continuing at the cemetery. "We have a nice life."

It's clear they miss their son, although they are happy to have their three daughters, Susan, Bonnie and Sharon Cameron, working with them part-time. Bill reminisced about how much fun it was sleeping at the cemetery with his son on Halloween nights, "for security purposes. People would climb over the walls, drinking and drugging. But that doesn't happen so often now. And we have guards who drive people out."

Nevertheless, he added, "We get our share of crazies, being in the heart of the city. A guy with fake jewelry threatened to shoot me when I wouldn't buy any. My son Billy pointed a shotgun at him and the guy ran."

Another time a man was screaming in the street outside. "He lunged at Joan with a knife. She gave him a well-placed kick!"

"Oh yeah, he got close," she said. "Too close."

They told me some other great stories, such as the day a funeral director forgot to show up for the service and Bill had to calm down 75 angry people until the director sped in. Another time a priest didn't show up because he fell asleep. Bill had to call him and wake him up.

"Once we had a casket from Italy," he recalled. "They glue on the handles instead of bolting them. As we got to the grave, the handles snapped off and the casket tumbled into the grave." (Fortunately, the body did not tumble out.)

Then there was the time Joan got trapped in a grave. "It was so deep, I couldn't get out. I was calling for help. I was buried up to my knees. A few more feet and that would have been it!"

Bill attends every funeral, "to make sure everything goes OK. You never know what might happen. We've had people try to jump into the graves."

Joan admitted, "It is kind of morbid sometimes. It bothers me when I've sold a grave to somebody and they die. Or when we bury young people."

When I asked Bill who might take over when they finally retire, he replied, "I have no idea. God help them! You have to be compassionate and dedicated."

"You have to care," Joan said.

Then I asked Bill how much longer he figures they will continue. "I think I'm good for another 10 years," he said.

"Sure!" she added. "Why not?"

And as you must know, they have their own plot there.

60

A Tip of the Hat to Walter Dudar, a Register Legend

(August 28, 2015)

WALTER DUDAR WAS THE LAST OF THE GREAT WALK-AROUND-TOWN newspapermen. Throughout the 1940s, '50s, '60s, '70s and even into the '80s he held a variety of downtown reporter beats and editor jobs at the *New Haven Register*.

Dudar, who died last Friday at 89 (services will be private), was a hometown guy: born in New Haven, raised in an apartment in the Legion Avenue neighborhood, educated in local schools. Then he dedicated his working life to writing about his city, which he covered like it was a small town.

Oh, he had his quirks; he never learned how to drive. He overcame this by taking advantage of the *Register*'s then-downtown location on Orange Street—hailing buses, trolleys and taxis when absolutely necessary and walking, walking, walking.

When you look at the reporters and editors in today's newsrooms, you can quote Dorothy in "The Wizard of Oz": "My! People come and go so quickly here!"

But not Walter Dudar. He was here to stay.

One day in the mid-1940s, shortly after he graduated from high school, he talked his way past the *Register*'s receptionist, walked upstairs and persuaded the managing editor to hire him, based on his drive and some clippings from his high school newspaper.

He didn't have enough money to go to college, he once told me. He said the Depression drove his dad's mattress company out of business.

"He couldn't afford to send me to college," Dudar said. "So I had to learn by the seat of my pants."

But after he quickly rose through the ranks, becoming city editor when he was just 29, Dudar helped many young reporters by showing them around town and teaching them the basics of good newspaper work.

John ("Jack") Quinn, who worked alongside Dudar for many years, noted this generosity in an Elm City Clarion column in August 2004, 18 years after Dudar retired. Quinn called him "a legendary newsman."

"Walter gave his all to the *Register*, fellow staffers and his reading public," Quinn wrote.

"I first met Walter back around 1950 at the off-duty hangout for area newsmen: Ed Malone's Three Steins Restaurant at Church and Grove streets," Quinn recalled.

"He was at that time the other half of an energetic and bustling police beat. He took the arrest info over the phone from another newspaper legend, Jimmy Molloy, a prototypical fedora-wearing police reporter-legman, and transformed it into a most interesting crime story."

Quinn said Dudar was "the best rewrite man in the business." Equally important: "His facts were always accurate."

"Walter Dudar was always around when needed," Quinn added. "He took many cub reporters under his wing and showed them the ropes. He saw them come and go as he went about his own newsroom duties. He was a loner of sorts but a friend to all."

Quinn wrote that column because he said Dudar needed "a little cheering up" after two major surgeries on his leg (it had to be amputated).

But Quinn noted Dudar was "in good hands" because several years earlier he had ended his longtime bachelorhood and married another former Register reporter and editor, Diana Zavras.

Dudar also needed his wife's support because he had lost his older brother Steve, who died from a heart attack. The two brothers had lived together for many years in an apartment on Orange Street. Big brother drove his little brother around town.

I had known Dudar as an older colleague of mine in the newsroom during the late 1970s and early-to-mid '80s. We kept in touch after he retired and we became friends after his brother died.

Seeing that he needed help getting here and there (this was before he got married), I started chauffeuring him around the area. I helped him get his groceries at the supermarket, pick up his dry cleaning at Jet Cleaners (he continued to wear ties and dress shirts, as if he were still working) and medical supplies. We had many lunches together, usually at his longtime favorite eateries: Jimmies of Savin Rock and Nick's Char Pit.

Even then he was full of tips about what was going on and provided me with story leads. He maintained a keen interest in New Haven's people and businesses, using his background and connections as the *Register*'s former business editor to dig out fresh nuggets for me.

And what a memory! As Zavras noted, "Walt was a walking encyclopedia of major state news events."

Although his health declined in recent years, forcing him to use a wheelchair and end his lifelong habit of walking all over town, he never complained or seemed depressed. His wife marveled at this, as did his doctors and nurses.

A longtime nurse who had watched his health fade away asked him why he was never angry or downhearted. He simply shrugged and replied, "What for?"

His wife told me another story about his upbeat outlook amidst the ongoing medical requirements. After an unexpectedly long hospital lab procedure, he came back to his room on a stretcher and announced: "It's a boy!"

It's too bad that many people in the New Haven area, including the great majority of my colleagues and most of the readers of this newspaper have never heard of Walter Dudar. But the older folks around town and in this newsroom do remember him and know full well what he contributed.

I will miss him as a friend and a father figure.

Everything's Good For Barber
Carl and His Customers

(November 29, 2015)

CARL MCMANUS WAS IN HIS ROOKIE YEAR, THE NEW KID IN FROM HOP-kinton, Mass., when he auditioned at Phil's Barber Shop on New Haven's Wall Street.

"He's from Boston and he's Irish!" said the new owner Rocky D'Eugenio to the former owner Phil Catania.

"I've never heard of a good Irish barber yet," Catania grumbled.

"So I gave him a haircut," McManus recalled. "And we became friends."

That was back in the fall of 1965. And McManus has been there ever since. Yes, if you're keeping score, that's 50 years.

During that time a parade of unforgettable personalities have come through the door and sat in those worn old chairs: Yale presidents, future U.S. presidents, famous actors and local characters.

It was a lucky series of events that brought McManus from Hopkinton—the town where the Boston Marathon has its starting line—to New Haven and the periphery of Yale University.

"I was stocking shelves and bagging groceries at the market in Hopkinton," McManus told me last Tuesday afternoon when I stopped in to hear his stories. "The butcher liked to play the horses running at Suffolk Downs. On Saturdays I'd bring his choices over to the barber, who was the bookmaker.

"One day I sat there and observed him. The atmosphere was very friendly, the kibitzing back and forth with the customers. I thought, 'Gee, I might want to do this kind of work.' So I went to the Massachusetts School of Barbering in Boston."

McManus got a job at a barber shop in that city. But after his father, a salesman for General Electric, got transferred to Bridgeport and bought a house in Milford, Carl's brother started pestering him about joining them in Connecticut.

"He told me, 'Oh, Mom's worried about you being alone,'" McManus said. "So I made the move. Still, I wanted to be on my own, so I lived above the barber shop here. There were a lot of bums, derelicts and drunks upstairs. But they were nice people."

McManus got to be friendly with an older barber in town who worked at The Graduate Club. McManus noticed he had a photo near his work bench of a pretty young lady; it was the barber's daughter. When McManus expressed an interest in meeting her, the elder barber set up a date. His daughter, Ethel, was dubious about the idea but her dad told her: "He's a nice clean-cut guy."

Within a year they were married. They have been together for 43 years and have a daughter, Rose, described by McManus as "beautiful inside and out."

There have been some rough patches with the barbering business during McManus' five decades. He shakes his head while remembering the darkest days, the 1960s and early '70s when "you had the long hair, the hippies. If it weren't for the people at the phone company (Southern New England Telephone), Rocky would've put the key in the door" and gone out of business.

But then one day, there was hope. McManus said it was around 1970. "Rev. Coffin (the Rev. William Sloane Coffin Jr., Yale's chaplain) came in and told us, 'Sharpen your shears. I just came back from England and shorter hair is back.' It took a few years to happen here but he was right."

Meanwhile, Yale went co-educational and Phil's Barber Shop became Phil's Hair Styles to accommodate women. Through the years New Haven has had more than one Phil's operating at the same time; today there is

Carl McManus at Phil's Hair Styles. (*New Haven Register* photographer Arnold Gold)

a second one on Whitney Avenue in New Haven, operated by Pasquale DeSisto and his brother Silvio.

McManus told me his boss, Pasquale, "is easy-going. The only thing he expects of us is raking in the dough."

DeSisto knows better than to tamper with anything on the walls of the Wall Street shop. The décor reflects McManus' lifelong obsession with the Boston Red Sox and his love of Yale. There is a framed photo of former President George H.W. Bush as well as assorted photos of Yale sports teams from as far back as the 1930s. Red Sox slugger David Ortiz has his photo and statistics on that wall and there's a collage of shots showing Red Sox pitcher Pedro Martinez doing his infamous takedown of Yankee bench coach Don Zimmer during the 2003 American League Championship Series.

One of the first things McManus showed me after I arrived was a card signed by many of his loyal customers, including former Yale President Richard C. Levin and current President Peter Salovey. One of the signers was "George Steinbrenner," the late Yankees owner. "Cheever Tyler wrote that," McManus said, referring to the New Haven civic leader.

"Jim Farnam asked me if I had ever been to a World Series game. I said no and, lo and behold, he got the guys together and they all contributed to get me two tickets to a game in the 2013 World Series! What a wonderful gift."

I asked him if the Sox won that night. "No, they got beat. But they won the World Series."

He gave me a meaningful look, knowing I'm a Yankees fan. I was in his shop for an earlier column in September 2004, listening to McManus and D'Eugenio, a passionate Yankees booster, banter over who was going to win that year. The following month, when the Red Sox finally broke "the curse of the Bambino," D'Eugenio "half-heartedly shook my hand," McManus recalled.

D'Eugenio died two years ago, McManus noted. "Rocky was a perfect gentleman."

Now McManus' only co-worker of his generation is Anthony Cavaliere, who for many years had a shop on Orange Street. But he has logged just three years so far on Wall Street.

Periodically, during my visit last week McManus kept bringing up that World Series gift from his customers. "Randall, who does that? To get all those people together!"

He became somber as he told me, "I want to thank my loyal friends, the Yale faculty, the Yale alumni. I can't express how kind they have been to me over the years. It gets to me sometimes when I think about it."

One of McManus' regulars and a signer of the gift card, the prominent attorney Hugh Keefe, told me: "Carl is an extremely popular barber. People will wait in a back-up line for him because he's such a good guy. He's a good barber too, but that's way down the totem pole."

Keefe added, "If he wanted, Carl could be the best police informant in town. He knows everything that's going on—who's getting divorced, etc. But he's like a good bartender; he keeps his mouth shut. He doesn't have a mean bone in his body."

Keefe has been getting his haircuts at Phil's for 35 years. But last Tuesday a young man walked in for the first time: Kevin Hwang, a Yale junior from Athens, Ohio. McManus got down to work. Bobby Vinton's "Blue Velvet" played in the background.

While he was cutting, McManus reminisced about his famous customers through the years. "Eli Wallach, he was a sweetheart of a guy. Hal Holbrook, he was very nice, and so was John Lithgow. They were in here when they were at Long Wharf (Theater)."

But Richard Dreyfuss was not so nice. "He was kind of a hard-ass."

"Rocky cut George H.W. Bush when he was a student here," McManus continued. "The younger Bush (George W.) never came in."

The student spoke up. "You've been cutting hair for 50 years? Long time." He is 19.

I noted McManus has an earring in his left ear and long locks. "I have the girls here cut my hair. I'm like you, Randall; I don't get it cut too often."

He is 72 and in no hurry to retire. "I'll go as long as I can. I'm not gonna be like Rocky though. He worked here for 70 years! Imagine that.

"I've been blessed working here. I consider the Yale community my second family. I've enjoyed every minute of it. I wouldn't want to work anywhere else but Phil's on Wall Street. When I hear my customer come in the door, it lights me up. Everything's good."

62

Hot Grill, Warm Heart Help
Jimmy Weather the Days

(January 17, 2016)

WHEN I APPROACHED JIMMY NIGRETTI AT HIS HOT DOG CART OUTSIDE
New Haven City Hall on Church Street last Tuesday afternoon, the tem-
perature was about 30 degrees, the wind was whipping down the sidewalk, there was no sun overhead and eating a wiener was the last thing
on my mind.

But when he saw me, Nigretti smiled and called out, "Whoo! It's
warming up now!"

What else could I do but smile back at him while taking in the
assorted signs he keeps plastered all over his stand. Perhaps the funniest
one is "Hot dog genius."

When I asked him about that one, he said, "I've kind of mastered it.
I'm good at it. I've earned it after being out here for 12 years."

Nigretti isn't the only hot dog vendor who is working through the
winter. You can see them at other parts of the New Haven Green and
in front of the courthouses. But what got me interested in Nigretti was
watching him push that heavy cart down the Orange Street sidewalk on
the many mornings I drive down to the state Superior Court building.

I asked him where he picks it up to begin his journey. "Oh, I keep it in
a garage I rent near the (New Haven) Lawn Club, by Humphrey Street.
It's about a mile down and a mile back."

He told me he doesn't mind doing that; it helps keep him healthy.

HOT Jimmy Nigretti at his hot dog cart outside New Haven City Hall. (*New Haven Register* photographer Peter Hvizdak)

"Everything is connected to the cart," he said. "My happiness, my health, humans, everything. I love people.

"This is what I love to do," he added. "It's easy for me. So easy!

"Nothing bothers me when I'm working. Not the weather, nothing. Work is therapy for me."

Nigretti feels it's important for him to be there. "I greet a lot of people. I'm like the downtown greeter."

He rarely misses a day's work, but even Nigretti gets sick sometimes. "One time I was out sick for two weeks. When I came back, everybody asked, 'Are you OK? You OK?' It makes me feel good.

"I'm just like Tiger Woods—people pay me to show up. They want me to be here. I'm here to help, you know what I mean? I give people directions, I give them a good word. It's all about respect."

Nigretti pointed to his "People before profits" sign. "I'm not out here for the money. It's only $2 for a hot dog; $5 gets you two dogs and an ice cold drink. It's about convenience, good food and a good word." (If you want to splurge, he'll sell you a large "Georgia hot" for $3.50.)

He often shouted, "Hey, buddy!" as folks passed by. When two guys stopped for dogs, he took care of business, then told them, "There's my cafeteria! Sit down and relax." He pointed to a stone slab bench in front of the Connecticut Financial Center. His customers laughed and kept going, doubtless on their way to a warm indoor place to eat their dogs.

Then Nigretti encouraged *New Haven Register* photographer Peter Hvizdak to take a break and sample one. "Have it 'my way.' That's with brown mustard, onions, chili and cheese. It's all about flavor. People like good food, you know?"

Hvizdak liked it.

Nigretti has had some memorable customers through the years. He recalled that while a big corruption (or worse) trial was happening at the federal courthouse just down the street from his cart, "The mobster guys pulled up here in a Mercedes. And they bought hot dogs from me! I was shaking in my boots."

He lives in Hamden but doesn't like hanging out there. "I stay out of the house as long as I can. If I'm home, I start eating, sleeping, watching TV. It's not healthy."

Nigretti, who is 52, lives alone. He has been married twice. "My first one lasted 19 years. I still love her. You know the first time you fall in love? Ain't nothing like it! I'm trying to get that again. I miss it. I've been by myself for about 10 years.

"I'm a chef by trade. I worked at a Chinese restaurant for eight years and at a steakhouse for six.

"For 18 years I was a bricklayer," he added. "I've got the best hands in the business."

But then he said, "I could never work for anybody again."

The wind was really picking up, rattling his big umbrella. "When the wind ricochets off these buildings," he said, "it gets really brutal out here. I'm in the wind tunnel."

My fingers were so cold that I pulled out my gloves. Nigretti flashed me a tolerant smile.

"I'm not cold at all!" he said. I checked out what he was wearing and I saw he was all layers: blue jeans with sweatpants pulled over them; two sweaters, with a sweatshirt on top of that. "Your legs are like heaters," he said. "And I'm not cold when I'm making money."

But then Nigretti said something that made me realize he's human after all. "When I leave here I go to the gym and jump in the sauna. My muscles need that after the cold. I go to the sauna for the deep heat. Ain't nuthin' like deep heat."

He also admitted something else: "I watch the weather like a farmer. If it's in the single digits and the wind's blowing, I don't want nothing to do with it. Plus, everybody stays inside anyway. If it's like that, I stay home."

It's clear this is no way to make a steady living. Nigretti told me he pays $200 every year for his vendor's license and $280 more annually for a health sticker, which he gets after a health inspector thoroughly checks out his equipment and procedures. But when I asked if he's making any money from this job, he shrugged and said, "I'm OK. I've got something to do."

I noticed he was munching on sections of apples. "I eat fruit all day long. And I eat a lot of oatmeal at home at night. Keeps me healthy."

Doesn't he eat his hot dogs? "I'll eat one once in a while. I'm tired of eating hot dogs."

Being out with the human race all day long has helped Nigretti develop a philosophy about people: "There's good and bad spirit transfers. You're a good one. When the bad ones come over here, I know it right away. Those ones that give me a bad time, they make me smarter. They're my best teachers.

"Anger is one letter short of danger. Anger is a luxury you can't afford. I can't get mad out here."

Naturally he offered me a hot dog. I usually eat hot dogs only when I'm in Yankee Stadium or Fenway Park but I took him up on his offer. He served me up a chili dog and I took a bite. Good stuff! Hot!

I thanked him and ducked into the warm alcove of City Hall to finish it off. Nigretti was still out there, with about another hour to go until quitting time and that long slog back up Orange Street.

63

The Amazing Walter Kaylin,
Already a Legend

(March 12, 2017)

WHEN I PICKED UP THE ASHES OF MY FATHER-IN-LAW, WALTER KAYLIN, last Monday morning at the crematorium in Wallingford and drove back to New Haven with him beside me, I thought about his wonderful life and his never-ending stories.

Listen, you would have to expect vivid, funny stories from a guy whose wild tales were in anthologies entitled "He-Men, Bag Men & Nymphos" and "Weasels Ripped My Flesh."

Walter wrote those during the late 1950s and '60s for pulp magazines such as "For Men Only," "True Action" and "Stag."

He spun sagas of macho men on dangerous tropical islands rescuing buxom damsels and plugging the bad guys. Many of these were war-related. Check out the title of his contribution to "Men" magazine, July 1966: "The Black Lace Blonde, the Yank Jungle Fighters and the Chicom Plot to Grab the Mid-Pacific."

Walter's colleagues in that New York City office included other tough-nut writers such as Mario Puzo, who would go on to write "The Godfather" and Joseph Heller, who later wrote "Catch-22."

Bruce Jay Friedman, another of Walter's peers, noted Walter was nothing like the characters he concocted.

"He looked like a divinity student, always buttoned up," Friedman recalled on the backside of one of Walter's anthologies. "Then the stories

would come in. They were special—seamless and outrageous
and wonderful. I think of him as
a treasure."

But Walter didn't achieve the
literary fame accorded to those
other writers. His two novels, "The
Power Forward" and "Another
Time, Another Woman" didn't
sell and quickly went out of print.

But at the age of 92, when
he was living at Apple Rehab in
Guilford, unable to walk, Walter
saw those two anthologies get
published, thanks to pulp fiction enthusiasts Robert Deis and
Wyatt Doyle.

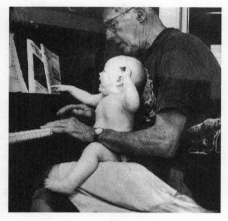

Walter Kaylin at his home in Old Lyme
with his granddaughter Charlotte Beach.
(Photo by Jennifer Kaylin)

"It means a lot to me," Walter told me when I asked him how it felt
to finally get such recognition.

But he never took himself too seriously. He added with a sly smile, "I
was reading those stories in bed last night and I was shocked at how savage they were. I was thinking: 'My God! Could this be me?'"

Walter got a lot of his source material during World War II, when
he was a radio operator in the Signal Corps of the U.S. Army, stationed
in the Philippines. He didn't see much combat but he met a lot of unforgettable guys and "dames." He recalled the women were gorgeous, "all of
them with mouthfuls of gold teeth."

Because Walter grew up in the Bronx near Yankee Stadium, he
watched Babe Ruth and Lou Gehrig in action. When Gehrig was mired
in a batting slump, Walter wrote him a letter, telling him not to worry,
that the hits would start coming again. Gehrig responded with a polite
thanks. I wish Walter had held onto that reply. But he certainly remembered it well.

Even when he was in his 90s, in a bed or his chair at the Guilford
rehab center, he could still recall seeing those fabled Yankees and others of

that era—Jackie Robinson, Willie Mays—playing for the local ball clubs. He also told us he saw Satchel Paige pitch when that star in the Negro leagues finally got a chance to play in the majors.

Walter and his wife, Peggy Kaylin, loved living in New York City but they also enjoyed getting out of town with their young daughters, Jennifer (the woman I would marry) and Lucy. In the late 1950s, they began to spend weekends in a beachside cottage in Old Lyme. Eventually, they got weary of the Sunday-night drives back to the city and they moved to Old Lyme to live there year-round.

But Walter never stopped writing. Jennifer recalls hearing him typing away in a room adjacent to the kitchen. Later he set up an office upstairs where he had an expansive view of the shoreline.

When he wanted to take a break from his writing he walked into the sun room on the first floor, sat down at the piano and played in his unique style: a rolling, rollicking, free-wheeling boogie woogie outpouring that was delightful.

During his four years at Apple Rehab, he kept a succession of typewriters in his room and he was constantly thinking of story ideas, then getting most of them down on paper.

We have been sorting through his many correspondences and story fragments and we came upon a letter he wrote to an editor at The New Yorker magazine.

"At age 90 I'm working on a highly unusual novel," he wrote. "'Hear the Chant of the Jungle' centers on the relationship between 23-year-old Paulie Ohlbaum of the Bronx and a considerably older, incredibly tall Watusi woman, Roz, who emerged from Rwanda (Congo) to take care of him for the first two years of his life, then disappeared and has rematerialized 20 years later. By this time Paulie and his older brother Luther own and run a motel, The Owl's Eye, in Connecticut, on the Sound."

Walter went on for a couple of pages, continuing to weave the imaginative scenario. He concluded the letter: "Does this interest you? If so, I'd be happy to send you the first section, which concludes with Roz getting set to meet Paulie for the first time in 20 years."

We couldn't find the editor's response, if there was one. But it didn't seem to matter much to Walter. He kept writing anyway, up until the final week or two of his life. That's an inspiration for all of us to keep going.

He also kept playing the piano. Apple Rehab has a community room where residents gather and there's a piano in the corner. Walter spent a lot of time seated there in his wheelchair, entertaining everyone within earshot.

Over the last year or two, Walter would sometimes hold up the bent, arthritic fingers of his right hand and complain he couldn't play piano as freely as he had in previous years. But that never stopped him.

He loved movies, especially the classics from his prime. A month or two ago my wife and I went to Best Video and rented "The Treasure of the Sierra Madre" for him. We watched it together at Apple. After it ended, Walter exclaimed, "That was some picture!" It would be the last one he ever saw.

We also supplied Walter with Heaven Hill, his favorite Bourbon whiskey. He always enjoyed a little glass of it just before dinnertime.

That community room, and I'm sure all of Apple Rehab itself, is quieter now, some of the life gone out of it. There are many people, besides us, who miss hearing Walter play and miss his stories.

His four grandkids, who he was so proud of, also dearly miss him. My younger daughter Charlotte posted a message that ended: "Papa, the world is already a little less cool without you."

He made it to 95. As he told us in his final year, he had done enough. He was ready to go. His wife had died in 2010.

Walter had few regrets; he didn't dwell on such stuff. He had enjoyed life. For many years, he sat with Peggy on the beach, sipping cocktails while listening to his jazz records playing from inside their home. As he watched the sun slowly set over the water, Walter always said, "It doesn't get any better than this."

One day this spring we will scatter his ashes in that idyllic playground where life couldn't get any better.

64

How "Carm" Cozza Became Like a Big Brother to a Register Newsman

(January 14, 2018)

ON JANUARY 4, WHEN BOB BARTON LEARNED FORMER YALE HEAD FOOT-ball coach Carmen Cozza had died, he thought back on their long association and the close bond they entered into after many years of knowing one another.

Barton, now retired, who wrote about Yale sports in addition to wearing many other hats as an editor at the *New Haven Register* for decades, at first had a necessarily removed, professional relationship with Cozza, winner of 10 Ivy League championships from 1965 through 1996.

"I think, as time went on and I kind of kept a respectful distance and didn't write everything I saw and heard, Carm appreciated that," Barton told me last Thursday when we met at Mory's, the storied New Haven restaurant long affiliated with Yale and its sports legends.

"Carm, I think, came to regard me as a friend in the media who could be trusted not to blab," Barton said as he sipped his coffee.

Barton, a 1957 Yale College graduate, has an encyclopedic knowledge of Yale football. He regaled me with stories of long-ago games and colorful players, replete with statistics. But after a while his tone became more serious.

"There came a time when Carm and I began to relate outside of football," he said.

Bob Barton beside a photo of Carmen "Carm" Cozza at Mory's restaurant. (*New Haven Register* photographer Catherine Avalone)

"In the winter of 2001-02—I think it was in March 2002—Carm was down in Florida and he was not feeling well," Barton noted. Cozza and his wife Jean spent their winters there.

"He felt so unwell that he decided to drive himself to the hospital. He told me Jean handed him six baby aspirins. When he got to the hospital he pulled up outside the emergency room, walked in and told the nurse on duty how he was feeling. The nurse said, 'Mr. Cozza, I think you're having a heart attack.'"

He was immediately admitted to the hospital. Barton tossed off another insider's anecdote: "The doctor said to Carm, 'You don't know me but I roomed with one of your players. We'll take good care of you.'"

Soon afterward Cozza had triple bypass surgery.

Barton proceeded to chapter two. "In September of 2003 I remember I felt funny after attending the (New Haven) Ravens' last game at Yale Field. I went to see my doctor. He told me, 'There's a cardiologist with an office downstairs. I am making you an appointment. Be there tomorrow morning.'"

The cardiologist did a test. "Yeah, I had had a heart attack," Barton told me. The surgery came shortly after that.

"When I next saw Carm, I told him, 'Carm, I've got something in common with you. I just had a triple bypass.' He said, 'Whatever your medical plan provides for in terms of rehab, do it. They know what to do to bring you back, to help you recapture the mobility and feeling whole again.'

"After that we had a bond. He was like a big brother to me. He was six and-a-half years older and he'd already been through it. He really cared. Once he knew I'd had this, he was there for me."

During our wide-ranging conversation at Mory's, we of course got around to "The Tie," a low point of Cozza's career. In the 1968 season finale against rival Harvard, the undefeated Yale team, playing at Harvard Stadium, had what seemed to be a comfortable lead of 29-13 with just three and-a-half minutes remaining. But unbelievably, the Crimson team capitalized on a Yale fumble, a recovered onside kick, two touchdowns and two two-point conversions (as well as perhaps some questionable calls by the referees) to score 16 points just before the game ended.

The famous Harvard Crimson headline blared: "Harvard Beats Yale, 29-29." For the Yale players and for Cozza and his staff as well as for the shocked Yale fans, it indeed felt like a loss.

At that point in our discussion, Barton reached into a bag and pulled out a yellowed edition of the Boston Globe, dated November 25, 1968, two days after the debacle. He pointed to a column on page one, head-lined: "Disappointed Yale Coach Questions Penalties."

Barton told me a UPI reporter called Cozza at about 7 a.m., the Sunday of that awful weekend, perhaps awakening him. Rather than hang up, Cozza answered the reporter's questions honestly, Barton said.

"When Carm saw the Globe had taken that and made this whole litany of objections out of it, I think he became gun-shy with the media almost ever after," Barton said.

And yet he noted Cozza remained patient and polite with reporters. "I could ask Carm any question and he would not make me feel like a fool for asking it. Some coaches will say, 'Why would you ask me such a dumb question?' Carm never said to me, 'Bob, why are you asking me this?'"

I asked Barton what made Cozza a good coach. "I think he was a teacher. And he did his best to surround himself with guys who could become good teachers. He knew how to sit back and let them teach."

Barton said Cozza became a father figure to his players. This came out in a story Barton wrote for the Yale-Harvard game program in 1993 in which he called Cozza "the pastoral counselor who deals with players one on one." He quoted Cozza: "We hope to give the kids some lessons about life."

Barton recalled a player saying: "Coach Cozza is like God. You don't want to screw up and get in trouble. Because if you do, you know he is going to land on you."

Barton told me about a player from a successful Yale freshman football team who celebrated by going out to a party. "Apparently he got howling drunk. I think he got into a sexual assault case. Carm got that kid into his office and told him: 'There are consequences for what you did and I can't ignore that. So you're not on the squad next year. But if you get things straightened out, we can talk about you coming back.'"

Barton noted, "The kid never played another down at Yale."

When I asked why Cozza had remained at Yale, turning down offers from universities with more prominent football programs, Barton replied, "I think Carm didn't want to take his three daughters out of school. I think he did what was good for his family."

Asked how it affected him when he received the news of Cozza's death, from complications of leukemia at 87, Barton said, "I hate to say this: I don't think it hit me emotionally. It hit me first as a newsman. That was my first impulse: 'What do I do as a newsman?'" He called around, making sure his contacts at newspaper sports departments knew Cozza was gone.

But then Barton told me, "Lately, I've kind of become mad at Carm for dying. Because I miss the guy. There is, no question, a vacancy in my psyche. I've lost a guy I could trust and a guy I could ask any football question on this green earth."

Barton added, "I wish I'd asked him hundreds more."

65

Tom Ullmann Leaves Us a Soulful Legacy

(April 20, 2018)

IF WE'RE LUCKY, IN OUR LIFETIMES WE COME ACROSS AND GET TO SPEND time with those rare people who light up a room when they walk in.

And sometimes those buoyant personalities also have the ability to inspire us with their idealistic work and beliefs. They make us want to do better ourselves.

Tom Ullmann was such a man.

That's why it's such a loss, his sudden and shocking death last Friday in a hiking accident in the Adirondack Mountains.

He was 67, with plenty more still to give.

I got to know Tom over the past 12 years while covering difficult criminal cases in New Haven Superior Court, where he headed the Office of Public Defenders. No matter how emotionally tough the situation— especially defending Steven Hayes, one of the two men convicted in the Cheshire triple homicide—Tom was always calm, empathetic and helpful to everybody around him, including me. He took time to answer all of my questions, to explain points of law or anything else.

He always acknowledged that Hayes and co-defendant Joshua Komisarjevsky committed horrible acts in the deaths of Jennifer Hawke-Petit and her daughters Michaela and Hayley. But he said giving everyone a fair trial is "a Constitutional imperative, part of the heritage we have in this country." Tom received at least one death threat during the Hayes trial.

Tom Ullmann in his incredibly messy office at the time of his retirement. (*New Haven Register* photographer Peter Hvizdak)

I think what I'll miss most of all about Tom is sitting with him in his unbelievably messy office, piled high with documents, where we talked about "our" New York Yankees.

When he told me three years ago he was planning to retire in 2017, I was saddened. But his explanation made perfect sense.

Although he said he still loved his work and would "miss it tremendously," something had happened that year (2015) which profoundly influenced his attitude about when to retire.

This is how he explained it during our interview for his retirement in September 2017: "A close friend of mine got sick out of the blue and he passed away within three months. I'm leaving before something catastrophic happens. I have a lot of things I want to do: hiking, kayaking, traveling with my wife, seeing our sons."

Those words have reverberated in my mind since last Saturday when I learned of his death.

His wife, Diana Pacetta-Ullmann, told Paul Bass of the New Haven Independent that Tom was excited about hiking a trial near their vacation home. He told her he would be back by 4 p.m.

By 5 p.m., she knew something was very wrong. She called New York state troopers, who that night found his body in a ravine.

I've been gathering comments over the past week from his devastated friends. All of them said they can't believe that such a strong, vital man is suddenly no longer here.

Rick Kaletsky told me he chatted amiably with Tom on Sunday, April 8 at a birthday party for Jimmy Wolf, Tom's close friend.

"As always, Tommy was absolutely affable," Kaletsky said. "Man, it was always right away, that smile on his face and the warm greeting. I can't absorb the concept of he and I were having this nice conversation and five days later, he's gone."

Wolf told me Tom was "the most compassionate person I've ever known." He recalled that as Tom was leaving the party, "He gave me a big hug and said he was going hiking in the Adirondacks. He was looking forward to a hiking trip in Finland next fall."

Attorney Hugh Keefe told me in an email: "I last saw Tommy around St. Patrick's Day and kidded him for not wearing any green. His retort was spot on: 'I don't need green clothes—I have an Irish soul.' And if having an Irish soul means helping the little guy out, being a master of self-deprecation and having a rapier wit, then Tommy indeed possessed an Irish soul. He was the personification of a great public defender who cared deeply for his underdog clients while never taking himself too seriously. Those of us who were very fond of Tom take comfort in knowing his soul, Irish or not, is resting in heaven, smiling at all the well-deserved accolades being paid him."

In the eyes of attorney William Dow III, "Tom Ullmann was the gold standard for criminal defense lawyers. His approach, conduct and professionalism is the standard against which all criminal defense lawyers judge themselves, and inevitably we come up short."

Dow added, "He ran the best public defender's office in New England and beyond. And he did that by the example he set. He fought for everybody and wouldn't back down."

Dow recalled Tom telling him: "I always had the Constitution on my side and that's all I needed."

Dow brought up what the rest of us have been thinking: "The irony here is he retired because he lost two friends too early—his male friend and 'Cookie' Polan." (She was another highly-respected New Haven defense attorney; she died in October 2016 after a long struggle with cancer).

Attorney Glenn Conway met Tom in 1995 when Conway was doing an internship for law school. "Tom was a busy guy but he took time to find out about me. He would always take time to explain everything. Not all lawyers are like that!"

Conway added, "You could sense this was an absolute true believer. He believed in what he was doing, he believed in the rule of law, he believed in a zealous defense, no matter what the circumstances—the Cheshire case being the best example. Stepping up to handle that was no small feat.

"When I think of Tom," Conway said, "I remember he always had that big, infectious smile. He was a very upbeat person. He maintained a good sense of humor in a tough business."

Beth A. Merkin, who succeeded Tom as head public defender in New Haven and was a close friend of his, struggled to control her emotions as she sat in her office with me and talked about him.

I asked about her first impression of him when they met at the courthouse in 1989. "He immediately caught my attention as somebody to look up to as a role model. When he was in court, the way he handled his clients' cases, it was wonderful to watch."

Merkin said she has received calls all week from those former clients. "They are heartbroken. It shows the depth of the relationships he formed with his clients. Even after a case was closed, the relationship was ongoing."

She played for me a recording of one of those messages. An elderly man said: "This is Tom's old client and his best friend."

Merkin noted this was the main thing about Tom: "He always made a connection."

She also remarked that despite all the time Tom devoted to his cases and his family, he still found time to teach at the Yale and Quinnipiac

University law schools. He taught at Yale's Criminal Justice Clinic for at least the past seven years.

"He felt it was really important to teach others and to help others," Merkin said. "He inspired so many young people to become public defenders. His mentorship, his ideals and his passion for the job is spreading. We've all grown and learned from him."

Merkin noted the New Haven Superior Court judges arranged to have the flags outside the courthouse flown at half-staff this week.

66

"Oldest Head Shop on Planet" Hits 50

(May 6, 2018)

WALK RIGHT IN. TAKE A DEEP BREATH, INHALE. AH, YES! INCENSE!

Listen! That's the Doors: "Strange days have found us . . ."

Now behold the tie-dyed T-shirts, the funky jewelry, the whimsical tchotchkes, the peace posters, pottery, candles and lava lamps.

And especially behold that perennially smiling man behind the front counter, he of the long-flowing gray beard.

For 50 years, Raffael DiLauro has effortlessly, so it seems, maintained that spirit of 1968 in his timeless "head shop," the Group W Bench.

If you don't recognize that name, let me tell you a story. On that fateful Thanksgiving Day of 1965, a young folk singer, Arlo Guthrie, went to Great Barrington, Massachusetts, to visit a friend, Alice Brock.

Guthrie and his friends decided to pay back Brock for that fine Thanksgiving meal. And so they took out the garbage. (It had piled up. It was considerable.)

Discovering that the town dump in neighboring Stockbridge was closed for the holiday, Guthrie and his mates came upon a ravine where some other folks had deposited their garbage. The Guthrie brigade thus added to that pile.

On the following day the soon-to-be-infamous "Officer Obie" tracked down Guthrie and arrested him for littering. This was followed by another fateful encounter, with the military draft authorities in New York City. As Guthrie sang/narrated in his epic "Alice's Restaurant Massacree," they

Raffael DiLauro at his Group W Bench. (*New Haven Register* photographer Arnold Gold)

made him sit on the Group W Bench because he wasn't "moral enough to burn women, kids, houses and villages after being a litterbug."

"Alice's Restaurant Massacree" was in the air when young DiLauro, who had had his own run-in with the military, got a general discharge from the National Guard. He opened his little shop, first located on Howard Avenue in New Haven.

I've known DiLauro for many of the ensuing 50 years, but never had he been willing to tell me exactly what happened when he went into the National Guard, a strategy to avoid being sent to Vietnam. However, when I was with him last Tuesday afternoon to talk about the Group W's 50th anniversary, he opened up.

"In basic training my body was saying, 'You don't belong here.' You know when you go against the grain? That's how I felt. I had to go see a shrink (as did Guthrie). He was working with the (war) resistance and he helped me get out."

Recalling his shop's early days, DiLauro said, "We were a hub for the counter-culture. It was where you went to bring your flyers or posters. A 'question authority' kind of thing."

As for adopting the Group W Bench name to signal the shop's mission and sensibility, I'll quote from what DiLauro told me when I interviewed him in 1987: "We were sitting outside the place one day early on, talking about a name for it. I was already thinking about calling it the Group W Bench. Then a woman came by and threw her garbage in the dumpster. She clinched it when she mentioned the song and Arlo's garbage. It felt natural."

But DiLauro's landlord didn't dig having all those hippies hanging around, so DiLauro moved to Edgewood Avenue. The neighbors there didn't dig hippies any more than did the Howard Avenue landlord, so DiLauro found a more tolerant block at 1171 Chapel Street, near Yale.

DiLauro is hazy about dates. When I asked him what year he moved to his current Chapel Street location, he scratched his beard, shrugged, smiled and said, "It was some time in the early '70s."

He was standing alongside a cash register that is like no other you will ever see. It's adorned with depictions of John Lennon and Jesus, as well as a postcard showing all of those hippies gathered together outside Group W in the early days.

There is also posted a button with this message: "No cell phones please. They disturb the atmosphere—Mother Earth."

Near that is a photo of Donald Trump, with the maxim: "Stupid lives matter."

Yes, and when I asked DiLauro if his shop is still relevant in 2018, he said, "Absolutely! More so than ever. It all came around again. 'Impeach Nixon' is now 'Impeach Trump.'"

I mentioned the store's 50th birthday sales days coming up next Wednesday through Friday and quoted Bob Dylan: "How does it feel?"

DiLauro laughed; he still laughs a lot. "I didn't think I'd be here at this point! Who would've thought that? We're lucky, though. Three, maybe four generations have shopped here now."

He said it's been fun but he added, "It's always been hard work. But the vibe helps."

Ah yes, "the vibe." DiLauro said, "I think it's lasted all these years because it's a comfort zone, a safety zone, where people can come and talk."

When I wondered how on earth he has weathered all the economic and social changes of the past 50 years and stayed in business, he replied in his usual simple way. "What I like and what I buy seems to have appeal. I don't know any more than that. I guess I'm a collector and I have a place to collect and sell. Dylan said the music was just coming through him; at times you're in touch with that vibe. I'm lucky I still have it."

He laughed. "It may never fade away!" Let's hope not.

DiLauro said he doesn't object to the term "head shop." "I often say we're the longest-running 'head shop' on the planet."

DiLauro did duck one question: his age. "I'm not telling! I'm sure somebody can figure it out." And again he laughed.

"I Feel Free" by Cream was playing as we spoke. "I made this tape for the birthday. Most of the songs are from 1968. This album saved my life when I was in the National Guard. That was the great thing about the '60s: the music. It was the center of everything that was happening. And we still have it! It'll never die."

DiLauro was preaching to the choir but I let him keep rolling. "It was the glue that kept people together. It was meaningful and it still is. It gives me chills."

When we headed out to a nearby coffee shop for more talking, we stepped around the sidewalk chalk art being drawn at the shop's entryway by Matt Vercillo, who has been working with DiLauro for eight years. Vercillo was drawing a bright yellow sun.

Over our coffee, DiLauro admitted, "I don't have as much energy as I did, obviously. I work less hours: five days a week. I'm gonna say I'm casual." (Vercillo often is the one behind the counter until DiLauro rolls in.)

The talk of shorter work hours led to the logical next question: what about the future of Group W Bench? How much longer does he want to carry on?

"Oh, that's a tough question!" he said. "That's almost scary to answer. You have to pass the torch, but can you? My business is so personal. As my mother used to say, you just put one foot in front of the other. That's all I'm doing."

DiLauro, who lives in Guilford and proudly told me he has four grandchildren, is also a painter. But he acknowledged, "I couldn't support myself on it."

The main thing DiLauro seems to like about being at Group W is "having time to converse. Look around—nobody converses!"

He gestured toward the people sitting hunched over their laptops and cell phones at the coffee shop. "Everybody's plugged in. It's like outer space! They're all 'on' something; they're not together. This is what I miss the most (about the '60s): people hanging out, talking."

I reminded DiLauro of something he said to me years ago, a lament I have often thought back on: "Nobody hangs out anymore."

"That's right!" he said when I brought up his quote.

When I asked DiLauro if he has ever met Guthrie, he said he rode around with him on Guthrie's "Blunder Bus" when he was doing a European tour. The dates are lost in time. "We drank all the beer we could."

I asked if Guthrie has ever been to DiLauro's shop. "I don't think so," he said, giving a thoughtful look.

Paging Arlo Guthrie: Get there, man! It's been 50 years! You can get anything you want . . .

67

Fun With My Buddy on the Radio

(August 30, 2019)

ON THE FIRST AND THIRD WEDNESDAY OF EVERY MONTH AT 9 A.M., IF
you tune your radio dial to 89.5 FM, you will hear the Ramsey Lewis
Trio's instrumental version of "The 'In' Crowd" (1965) and a DJ joyously
singing along with it, bopping his hands on a table and punctuating his
vocalisms with "Oh yeah!"

And that, my friends, is how Carl J. Frano, WPKN's longtime oldies
enthusiast, begins every show.

He's been entertaining and enlightening us for 29 years. As a fellow
fan of those rock 'n' roll oldies from the '50s and '60s, I have been listening
to him all these years. And finally last Wednesday I got my chance to be
a guest on his show!

We had been negotiating this for a long time. Frano is very, I must
say, *precise* in his approach. He meticulously prepares for every minute of
his three-hour show, down to the exact length of each song and how it fits
the particular theme of that week.

A few months ago, when Frano invited me on and listed the themes
of his upcoming shows, I chose August 21 because he was doing an all-
1964 extravaganza, focusing especially on summertime songs from that
year. I really liked 1964; I remember it fondly from my youth. The Beatles
arrived! The "British Invasion"!

And so early last Wednesday morning Frano drove down to Bridgeport and the tiny WPKN studio from his house in Guilford, where I

interviewed him in February 2018 (he adores Guilford) and I drove down from my home in New Haven.

He greeted me with his usual ebullience, then gave me a tour of the cramped rooms whose shelves are stuffed wall-to-ceiling with albums and CDs and still a few 45 r.p.m. records. WPKN is an independent community radio station dependent on listeners' donations; every DJ there does it for free, for the love of the music.

I had brought with me one of my cases of 45s, including Manfred Mann's "Do Wah Diddy Diddy," because it was from 1964 and, guess what, it was the first 45 I ever bought! I remember bopping around on a grassy field, my transistor radio to my ear, hearing that song and saying: "I must have it!"

Frano looked at that record with awe. "This is 55 years old!" he marveled. "We'll see what we can do to squeeze it in."

I had brought some other possibilities, including the early Rolling Stones song "Tell Me" because it, too, was from 1964. But Frano had his playlist all set and there would be nothing "squeezed in" except for, maybe, "Do Wah Diddy Diddy."

"Lor-dee!" Frano exulted as he scurried around the little studio where he does his show. He was getting ready for show time. Frano was dressed in a WPKN T-shirt and gym shorts because the air conditioning wasn't working and it was a tad hot in there. I sat down across from him, with access to my own microphone.

Before he went on the air, Frano made me a copy of that playlist: five pages of scrawled titles, including the month each song charted and the record label. The total number of records he was shooting to play: 54. Plus, if I was lucky, my "Do Wah Diddy Diddy."

Frano also showed me "my Bible," a tattered Billboard magazine book of all the songs that made the charts, going back to 1955. From that he had hand-written page after yellow page of song lists, part of his continuing education.

"Oh my God, it's time to do this thing!" he shouted, and ambled over to his seat and desk, surrounded by a turntable and other equipment. "I'm playing some vinyl today," he revealed. "A Beatles 45, 'From Me to You.'"

"We're good to go!" he told me. "The Carl J. Frano show is ready for take-off!"

Then he cued up "The 'In' Crowd" and off he went. "Good morning, everybody! This is Carl J. Frano, coming to you from WPKN, 89.5 FM, live-streaming at www.wpkn.org. It's time to kick off our last official summertime show. Today is the seventh year in a row I'm highlighting the songs of 1964, a wonderful year for oldies music: a mix of American tunes and the 'British Invasion.'"

Frano told his listeners he planned to also include some romantic Broadway show tunes. "I've had such a beautiful summer; I thought some nice love songs were in order."

Frano graciously introduced me and I in turn thanked him for having me on his show. I remarked what a privilege this was and how "fabulous" his show is. I chose that word because I've noticed it's Frano's favorite.

The fun thing about listening to Frano's selections is that, no matter how well you know the songs of that era (and I know 1964 very, very well), you will always hear something completely new to your ears. The third song on his list was "Journey to the Stars" by the Ventures. What? "From July 1964," Frano announced. "It did not chart. But it's a great Ventures song."

Great indeed. After he played it, Frano said, "Isn't that fabulous? Coming up: The Pixies Three, a very obscure band, with 'Summertime U.S.A.'"

He followed that with "Keep an Eye on Summer" by the Beach Boys and "Hey Da Da Dow" by the Dolphins. I had never heard those two songs either. I was being educated, along with everybody else out there.

Of course many of the songs on the list were wonderfully familiar. When Frano played "Please Please Me" by the Beatles, he cried out: "I love these early Beatles, even earlier than 1964." His notes showed they recorded that song in November 1962, but it didn't make it onto the American charts until February 1, 1964.

Frano reminded his listeners that President John F. Kennedy had been assassinated in November 1963. "The country was just shocked. I think all this beautiful music that was so uplifting was such a reaction to that."

As the show neared the end of its first hour, Frano kept a careful eye on the clock. He decided to eliminate Louis Armstrong's "Hello Dolly" and Dean Martin's "Everybody Loves Somebody" because of time constraints. But he did put on "Do Wah Diddy Diddy," with my introduction. Thanks, buddy!

"This is the actual 45 r.p.m. record," Frano told his listeners. "It was number one for two weeks in the fall of 1964."

I reluctantly headed back to New Haven before 12 noon, needing to do a little work. But I caught the rest of the show on my car radio. "Randy" by Earl Jean! (Never heard it before). "Muscle Beach Party" by Annette Funicello. And the closer: "She's Not There" by the Zombies.

Then we were hearing "The 'In' Crowd" one more time and Frano was saying goodbye, drive carefully, he'd see us in two weeks. Whee!

68

The O'Connell Legacy
Remains in New Haven

(September 1, 2019)

OUR STORY BEGINS IN THE MID-1950S AT THE A.C. GILBERT CO. ON Peck Street in New Haven, where Craig O'Connell's father, Walter O'Connell, worked as part of the vast toy-making operation.

Young Craig's dad often would walk with his son from the family's tiny flat in the "Goatville" section of the East Rock neighborhood to the factory, where he would show the boy the toys and the company's showroom, featuring a gorgeous, intricate model railroad layout.

For Christmas of 1957, when Craig was 10, his dad bought him his first train: the Keystone Rocket Freight, a Pennsylvania Railroad docksider replete with a rocket-launcher, gondola and caboose.

This led to a Saturday morning tradition of walking to A.C. Gilbert with his dad to buy a new piece of American Flyer equipment he could add to his collection.

Shortly afterward, the family moved from their cold water apartment to a house in nearby Newhallville.

"Our dream was to build a model railroad in our basement once we had our own house," O'Connell said. "But that never happened."

On February 16, 1959, 16 months after the move to that new house, O'Connell was working his usual shift in the paint and plating department, operating a de-greasing machine for rejected Gilbert products. His job required him to work in an enclosure next to two large tanks filled with toxic chemicals.

Craig O'Connell with his train layout in his Hamden basement. (*New Haven Register* photographer Christian Abraham)

At about 1 p.m. that day, O'Connell was overcome by the chemical fumes and fell into a vat of acid. His body was instantly destroyed. "Okie," as his co-workers affectionately called him, was just 38.

"My life fell apart the day he died," O'Connell said. "I grew up an angry kid."

And yet that long-dreamed-of model train layout was built in O'Connell's basement at his home in the Spring Glen neighborhood of Hamden. He's been working on it for 30 years. In more recent years, he built a second one.

"I dedicated this to my dad," O'Connell, now 71, said last Tuesday afternoon as he stood alongside the older and larger layout, a remarkably detailed and lovingly created work of art.

"He gave me his love of trains," O'Connell said. "And I passed it on to children as a school teacher."

During his 42 years of teaching at Lincoln-Bassett School, Martin Luther King Jr. School and St. Thomas's Day School, all in New Haven, O'Connell frequently would put together field trips, bringing his kids to his basement to behold his creation.

"I'd bring them here from the classroom and we'd run the trains," he said. "The kids would operate the accessories."

O'Connell's presentation to the students centered on teaching them what he calls "the art of illusion." He pointed underneath one of the train trestles. "That 'river' looks real; it looks like real water. You get the illusion of depth." He showed me the epoxy, painted black and green, that created this illusion.

Then he pointed to a small campfire with slight illumination. "That's an illusion too. And here's another illusion: these windows on this industrial building look pretty real, don't they? See what it looks like, a broken window? That's frosted scotch tape."

O'Connell walked a few steps to his right and showed me a miniature light tower. "This is Gabe the lamp-lighter." O'Connell pulled a switch and the tiny figure climbed the tower, turned the light on, then quickly slid down.

For 62 years O'Connell has held onto and carefully maintained that original Keystone Rocket Freight. He pointed out its rocket-launcher, then said, "Let's see if it goes."

Zoom! Wow!

"Kids would love to shoot the rocket and watch Gabe climb the tower," O'Connell said. "That was part of my explanation to them about having a passion for this and the artistic element. It was a learning experience."

Sometimes he would top off the field trip by having the kids ride on a real train—something that many of them had never before experienced.

He recalled living in Newhallville, a half-block from the Farmington Canal Railroad, which then ran close to Dixwell Avenue. (It's now a biking and pedestrian trail.) This also nurtured his love of trains. And he remembers standing on a fire escape on Court Street downtown, counting the cars on the trains as they passed to and from Union Station.

O'Connell walked over to his control board and started up the trains. As they wound around the tracks, he noted, "One is an Amtrak and the other is the Crescent, the Southern Railroad."

The layout includes some original toys from A.C. Gilbert, which long ago went out of business. Some of the fixtures were named after members of his family: Ann's Stardust Diner for his wife, Ann O'Connell; a